EDUCATORS' PASSPORT TO INTERNATIONAL JOBS

EDUCATORS' PASSPORT
TO INTERNATIONAL JOBS
How to Find and Enjoy Employment Abroad

053576
c.5

REBECCA ANTHONY & GERALD ROE

Peterson's Guides

Princeton, New Jersey

Library of Congress Cataloging in Publication Data

Anthony, Rebecca, 1950–
    Educators' passport to international jobs.

    Includes index.
    1. Educational exchanges. 2. Teachers, Interchange of.
I. Roe, Gerald. II. Title.
LB2283.A58 1984   370.19'63   83-25094
ISBN 0-87866-271-5

Printed in the United States of America

10 9 8 7 6 5 4 3 2 1

For Tas and Laurie,
who share our travels and adventures

Contents

Preface

Do you want to teach overseas?

Do you know how to begin your job search?

Do you need help with résumés? letters? interviewing?

Do you wonder if you can adjust to living and working abroad?

Educators' Passport to International Jobs can answer your questions about how to find overseas jobs, how to get hired, and how to get back home again. A comprehensive guide, this book can take you from your first tentative daydreams about foreign teaching through a step-by-step process of finding information, learning and applying effective job-seeking skills and strategies, preparing to live abroad and, finally, returning to stateside employment.

As career and placement specialists at The University of Iowa, we work with first-time job seekers and with experienced professionals whose educational preparation ranges from the bachelor's degree through the doctorate. In addition to helping job seekers, we assist hiring officials in their search for qualified candidates for teaching and administrative positions in elementary and secondary schools and in colleges and universities. We know that any job search can be lengthy, time-consuming, sometimes expensive, and nearly always frustrating at some point in its development, and that seeking a position in a foreign country can present even greater difficulties. We know, too, that not everyone who looks for an overseas job will find one, and that not everyone who accepts a position in a foreign country will find the experience satisfactory. This book has been designed to help you determine if you have the necessary qualities and characteristics to succeed in an overseas assignment and, should you decide to pursue international opportunities, to offer support and encouragement for the realization of your career goals.

Our first book, *From Contact to Contract: A Teacher's Employment Guide,* discusses and illustrates the various steps of the employment process in the United States. The idea for *Educators' Passport to International Jobs* began when we realized the need for a book addressing the unique concerns of educators seeking positions abroad. Although various publications provide lists of schools or embassies to contact, our book deals with all aspects of an overseas job search. Our contacts with teachers, administrators, and hiring officials around the world allowed us to draw on the experiences of educators currently working in foreign settings and on the experiences of those who have completed an overseas assignment and returned to the United States. Their comments, incorporated into each chapter, provide firsthand information, suggestions, and advice about international careers and will give you an idea of what life is like in various countries—both inside and outside the classroom.

We are sure the results of our efforts can assist you in exploring your options for an international career in education, and we hope you will find our book interesting, informative, and even enjoyable.

REBECCA ANTHONY
GERALD ROE

Acknowledgments

We wish to express our gratitude to the following people for their willingness to share their insights and reflections. Their candid, thoughtful observations, invaluable to us in writing this book, allow the reader to receive firsthand impressions of the employment process and of life in many different countries. And to Travis Montgomery and Donald Wood, for their efforts to promote and further the cause of international education, we are especially indebted.

Walid Abushakra
The Universal American School
Khaldiyah, Kuwait

Dr. Barbara Poston Anderson
Kuring-gai College of Advanced
    Education
Sydney, Australia

J. Chris Anderson
École Secondaire de Bulape
Bulape, Zaire

R. L. Ater
The International School of Brussels
Brussels, Belgium

Daniel Baker
Wesley College
Belize City, Belize

Patricia L. Ball
American International School
    of Vienna
Vienna, Austria

Donald L. Ballentine
Saudi Arabian International Schools
Dhahran, Saudi Arabia

Dr. James Braunger
Taipei American School
Taipei, Taiwan

Richard C. Chesley
American Cooperative School
Monrovia, Liberia

David Chojnacki
International School of Ouagadougou
Ouagadougou, Upper Volta

Sharon Chojnacki
International School of Ouagadougou
Ouagadougou, Upper Volta

John Clayton
Matsieng Development Corporation
Matsieng, Lesotho

Howard G. Collins
American Cooperative School
Monrovia, Liberia

Lyn K. Collins
American Cooperative School
Monrovia, Liberia

Michael E. Collins
ARAMCO Schools
Dhahran, Saudi Arabia

William C. Dailey
American School
Tegucigalpa, Honduras

John E. Dansdill
Southern Peru Copper Corporation
    Staff School
Ilo, Peru

Kathryn Duermyer
American School of Isfahan
Isfahan, Iran

William Duermyer
American School of Isfahan
Isfahan, Iran

Bruce R. Fehn
Pinewood Schools of Thessaloniki,
    Inc.
Thessaloniki, Greece

Dr. Gilbert Fernandes
Colegio Franklin Delano Roosevelt
Lima, Peru

Shirley Fernandes
Lima, Peru

Ellen Flaspohler
Université de Picardie
Amiens, France

Gary Goodell
International School of Brussels
Brussels, Belgium

Janice Guyer
ARAMCO Schools
Dhahran, Saudi Arabia

Floyd L. Hall
American Cooperative School
La Paz, Bolivia

Dr. Curtis C. Harvey
Colegio Bolivar
Cali, Colombia

Larry E. Hoffer
Saudi Arabian International Schools
Dhahran, Saudi Arabia

C. Patrick Hotle
Cairo American College
Cairo, Egypt

Philip G. Houseal
Southern Peru Copper Corporation
    Staff School
Ilo, Peru

Dr. Robert Iannuzzelli
The American School of Kuwait
Hawalli, Kuwait

Dr. Ross L. Iverson
American School
Tegucigalpa, Honduras

Curt Eric Jackson
Stavanger American School
Stavanger, Norway

Merritt B. Jensen
Nagoya International School
Nagoya, Japan

Kathleen L. Johns
American International School–Lisbon
Lisbon, Portugal

Joseph S. Kennedy
American School of Milan
Milan, Italy

Karen Leonard
Üsküdor American Academy for Girls
Istanbul, Turkey

David J. Losk
American School
Tegucigalpa, Honduras

Eugene McCoskey
American School of Brasilia
Brasilia, Brazil

Dr. Scott F. McNabb
Thammasat University
Bangkok, Thailand

Joy Miller
Lycée Municipal and Juvenat
    de St. Camille
Ouagadougou, Upper Volta

Thomas H. Mohr
Oil Company School
Tripoli, Libya

Dr. Alfrieta Parks Monagan
National Cultural Council
University of West Indies
St. Augustine, Trinidad
    and Mona, Jamaica

James Newmann
Colegio Franklin Delano Roosevelt
Lima, Peru

Dr. Gordon E. Parsons
Association for the Advancement
    of International Education
Gainesville, Florida

Acknowledgments

Milt Pavlina
Escola Maria Imaculada
São Paulo, Brazil

Dr. Herman J. Penland
American Cooperative School
La Paz, Bolivia

Steven Peterson
The Antwerp International School
Antwerp, Belgium

Padric M. Piper
Escola Americana de Belo Horizonte
Belo Horizonte, Brazil

Linda L. Reinhart
St. John's International School
Waterloo, Belgium

Michael Robinson
Cochabamba Cooperative School
Cochabamba, Bolivia

Dr. Thomas J. Rushcamp
Parents' Cooperative School
Jeddah, Saudi Arabia

David Samore
Colegio Karl C. Parrish
Barranquilla, Colombia

Theodore G. Schweitzer III
United Nations High Commission
    for Refugees
Geneva, Switzerland

John Stiles
International School of Brussels
Brussels, Belgium

Dr. Clifford H. Strommen
International School of Lusaka
Lusaka, Zambia

Holly Tancred
Rabat American School
Rabat, Morocco

Dr. Gary Theisen
Institute of Education
    and Teacher Training
Yogyakarta, Indonesia

Joseph L. Tresnak
Supreme Headquarters of
    the Allied Powers in Europe
American High School
(Department of Defense Dependents
    School)
Mons, Belgium

Richard F. Underwood
Seoul Foreign School
Seoul, Korea

Joel Wernecke
The American School of Barcelona
Barcelona, Spain

Robert L. Werner
International School of Yaounde
Yaounde, Cameroon

Dr. Charles West
National Conservatory of Peru
    and National Symphony of Peru
Lima, Peru

Ralph Whalen
Saudi Arabian International School
Riyadh, Saudi Arabia

Dr. Donald L. Wieber
American International School
    of Vienna
Vienna, Austria

Gail Zimmerman
American School of Kuwait
Hawalli, Kuwait

I was attracted by the opportunity to travel and to experience other countries and cultures in depth by living, working, and otherwise sharing aspects of daily life with indigenous people.

Lyn K. Collins
Monrovia, Liberia

Certainly, travel and adventure are great rewards, but perhaps most gratifying to me is working with educators from a diversity of backgrounds.

Clifford H. Strommen
Lusaka, Zambia

I've never made much money as a teacher, but I think teaching is indeed enriching in itself. Adventure is what you make of it, in or out of the classroom. Travel cannot but broaden one, as does meeting people whose thoughts and culture do not correspond with one's own.

J. Chris Anderson
Bulape, Zaire

I am using my profession to see the world.

Joel Wernecke
Barcelona, Spain

The cultural adventures, the exciting people, and having the world as your curriculum are an invaluable part of your life as an educator working abroad.

Donald L. Ballentine
Dhahran, Saudi Arabia

There are many rewards in teaching overseas, such as travel opportunities, observing different cultures, and meeting new and interesting people. I would have to list as one of the major advantages the school population itself. It is made up of intelligent, multinational students who are extremely easy and enjoyable to work with. The parents are very cooperative and supportive of the school.

Floyd L. Hall
La Paz, Bolivia

Chapter One

Why Go Abroad?

At some time or other, perhaps during that long second semester when the winter holidays have receded into a distant memory and summer seems impossibly far away, nearly every educator daydreams about travel poster images of exciting, exotic locations. Mediterranean beaches, tropical island sunsets, majestic mountain peaks, busy Oriental bazaars, or Norwegian fjords are not merely subjects for vacation dreams or fantasies of the good life; they are familiar realities for thousands of American educators who have chosen international careers. The opportunity to live and work overseas is not restricted to the lucky winners of some sort of international sweepstakes, nor, contrary to popular belief, do positions in desirable locations have to be inherited. The possibilities of finding professional employment in many different countries allow educators quite literally to work their way around the world.

Unquestionably, the experience of living and working in another country can contribute to personal growth and professional development, and many educators have found their international experiences immeasurably rewarding. Most have also experienced some degree of surprise, frustration, and disappointment. The purpose of this book is not to persuade educators to pursue a career overseas, but to assist those who are considering such opportunities to form realistic expectations, to make rational decisions, and to make the best use of their time, resources, talents, and abilities in the process of seeking a position.

Before embarking on a search for an overseas teaching, research, or administrative position, educators should seriously examine their motivations for going abroad. Drawing upon the experiences of educators at all academic levels, this chapter will outline some of the typical reasons educators consider overseas opportunities. The rewards to be gained from international experiences are balanced against some of the cautions expressed by veteran teachers and administrators.

SEEING THE WORLD

A primary motivation for many seeking an overseas position is the desire to travel more extensively than the average American educator can afford to do on a teacher's or administrator's salary. Many educators who decide to go abroad probably begin their job search with the thought expressed by Joseph L. Tresnak, currently teaching in Mons, Belgium: "I wanted to travel and needed an income at the same time." Whatever the location, nearly every overseas job offers fascinating opportunities for travel either within the host country or, during school holidays and vacations, within a radius of thousands of miles.

In conjunction with the opportunity to travel, the spirit of adventure often motivates educators to go abroad. Although advanced technology and media links have made most parts of the world at least superficially familiar, firsthand experience with another culture will still provide challenge and romance. The pleasures of unfamiliar surroundings and activities can be enjoyed in the relaxed atmosphere of a coffeehouse, in touring cathedrals or archaeological ruins, or in shopping for exotic items in crowded, noisy marketplaces. While the concept of adventure may differ with each person, the novelty of any new location can be refreshing and exhilarating.

Among professionals in general, educators are in an enviable position when it comes to their options for overseas relocation. They may choose to consider working in virtually any country of special interest, because there are career opportunities in education in nearly every corner of the world. If an educator's interests are less clearly defined, however, or the primary motivation is to experience a new location and culture, the exact site of employment may not be the major consideration. Karen Leonard, a teacher whose experiences have taken her to various parts of the world, suggests to people considering their first overseas assignment: "Unless you are extensively traveled, you are guessing whether you prefer to teach in Southeast Asia, South America, or Europe. The experience will be worthwhile even if it isn't exactly what you imagined."

Perhaps more than any other occupational group, professional educators are in a position to appreciate the value of travel as a learning experience. Even a brief visit to another country can be culturally and personally enriching, whether the traveler visits museums, historical monuments, and other sites of special interest or simply takes in the unfamiliar everyday sights and sounds of another country and another culture. As a tourist or temporary visitor, such experiences are invariably limited by self-imposed schedules and time constraints. Educators frequently cite the opportunity to immerse themselves more completely into another culture by settling into daily routines for extended periods as a basic motivation for working abroad and as a primary benefit of the experience. Gary Goodell, a teacher in Brussels, Belgium, says he was attracted to overseas teaching because "I wanted to see Europe in greater detail than I would if I were merely a tourist." Gilbert Fernandes, who spent two years teaching in Lima, Peru, defines living in a different culture as "the greatest reward" of his assignment, "something that the tourist can never experience."

The opportunity to become familiar with different cultures and to learn and use a foreign language is a benefit of working abroad which can extend to the educator's family as well. Curtis C. Harvey, administrator at Colegio Bolivar in Cali, Colombia, views his experience as an "opportunity to provide wider cultural experiences for my family members in preparation for the ever-expanding world they will enter."

Although an overseas assignment typically offers the educator virtually unlimited opportunities for exploration and adventure, it is important to keep in mind that all of these activities can be time-consuming, costly, and often exhausting. Just as in stateside teaching assignments, full-time attention must be given to one's professional duties, such as daily classroom preparations, homework planning and review, and extracurricular responsibilities. Steven Peterson, a teacher with experience in Europe, offers this useful reminder for new overseas job seekers: "International schools are looking for teachers, not travelers." Balancing professional responsibilities with the opportunities to explore new places is crucial to a successful and satisfying experience. Richard C. Chesley, Superintendent of the American Cooperative School in Monrovia, Liberia, addressed this topic in a paper presented at a recent conference of the African International Schools Association in Nairobi: "Occasionally, some teachers confuse priorities and place personal motives ahead of professional responsibilities. They lose sight of the fact that they are to sign or perhaps have signed a two-year contract to teach, not to set out on a two-year travel or tour omnibus."

ENHANCING PROFESSIONAL SKILLS

Living abroad offers educators numerous professional enrichments. Regardless of the level or discipline, teachers who spend a year or two in a foreign setting find a new enthusiasm and a fresh outlook on their subject matter and their profession. Among other rewards frequently identified by educators who have returned to stateside teaching positions after working abroad are a growth in self-knowledge and professional stature, a broader perspective on American society, the ability to help others who are interested in international education, and greater confidence in one's ability to teach brought about by firsthand experience with another culture.

Educators in many fields can directly enhance their professional skills through living and working abroad. In particular, teachers of foreign languages will benefit by spending a year or two among native speakers of the language. David Samore credits part of his success as a Spanish teacher in a Florida public school to his prior experience teaching in Barranquilla, Colombia: "It has been invaluable to my foreign language classes as a source of *realia* in the form of real-life anecdotes, examples, and illustrations." An English teacher specializing in British literature will undoubtedly profit from the opportunity to visit the actual places referred to in the *Canterbury Tales,* Shakespeare's plays, or the novels of Charles Dickens. Social studies teachers at both elementary and secondary levels can enrich and enliven their classes by taking their students on an imaginative whirlwind tour of foreign countries—displaying artifacts or wearing native costumes, showing slides, preparing authentic native dishes, demonstrating customary greetings, or sharing interesting words and phrases in common usage.

Educators at the university level may actually find it necessary to live and work in other countries in order to stay abreast of developments in their field of teaching or research, to have access to resource materials, to make contacts with colleagues, or to gain professional credibility. For example, specialists in the fields of anthropology or comparative education often must travel to various parts of the world to do fieldwork or research; frequently, they are able to combine their research with periods of teaching in foreign universities. Such experiences abroad can be a contributing factor in increasing employment possibilities in the United States or in improving chances for promotion and tenure.

The opportunity to experience another culture and to acquire or refine competencies in other languages can enhance instructional skills and educational backgrounds for educators at any level but can also contribute to the development of marketable skills for career changers. "I have visions of leaving the teaching profession and entering the business world," writes Patricia L. Ball. Her teaching experience in Vienna, Austria, has made it possible for her to learn another language in preparation for a new career.

LOOKING FOR GREENER PASTURES

The old saw about the grass being greener on the other side of the fence may influence some people to explore foreign careers. Educators at the elementary and secondary level may be attracted to international schools because of the appeal of working with a multinational faculty and student body, especially in a school with small classes of highly motivated students—as is frequently the case in international schools. Richard F. Underwood, Headmaster of Seoul Foreign School in Korea, comments: "The generally high calibre of students, the supportive attitudes of parents, the cooperative teamwork of the faculty and the school administration breed a sense of oneness, a unity of purpose often hard to find in the United States." Herman J. Penland, Superintendent of the American Cooperative School in La Paz, Bolivia, also speaks of the overseas American community's "positive outlook toward education and the cooperative attitude that exists between parents, students, and staff in the overseas school." Other

4

overseas educators have commented on the greater respect given teachers and administrators in international schools, and the fact that parents and students alike are appreciative of the time and effort put forth by the educational staff. According to Kathryn Duermyer, who has worked in schools in the Middle East: "Parents would thank me for teaching their children—something that doesn't happen too often in the U.S."

While living abroad can be a deeply rewarding experience for many people, it is a mistake to expect that personal or professional difficulties will disappear with a change of scene or to attempt to use a foreign career as a means of running away from problems or undesirable situations. In most instances, problems of depression or discontent, marital discord or romantic disillusionment, boredom or burnout are not diminished but intensified in unfamiliar surroundings. Karen Leonard, who has worked successfully in such disparate international settings as Chunju, Korea, and Istanbul, Turkey, advises: "If you don't like yourself, don't go. I was once told that living overseas doesn't change a person—only exposes the true person. It's nice to learn about yourself, but only if you can accept what you learn."

Individuals who are experiencing domestic problems may view the opportunity to go abroad as a means of liberating themselves from dissension and conflict. Sharing new experiences in a new location may sometimes temporarily alleviate tensions and bring people closer together, but Richard Chesley particularly warns against trying to repair a relationship by moving to a new situation: "People experiencing a marital problem are quite the same people in Barcelona or Ankara or Ouagadougou as they are in Miami or Detroit or Strawberry Point. People who have been experiencing marital difficulties have the added personal burden of adjustment which inevitably intensifies and complicates the problem." Chesley also counsels: "Except for the possibility of escaping the exuberant attentions of an overwrought mother-in-law or breaking the avaricious stranglehold of a free-spirited but unemployable brother-in-law, going overseas to escape a family problem is a mistake."

Another misconception is the belief that the novelty of working overseas will alleviate professional frustrations. In reality, an educator who is unhappy in a stateside assignment will, in most cases, find similar or even greater frustrations abroad. Whatever the view from the window, one classroom is pretty much like another, and, as Richard Chesley points out: "Regardless of what one has been led to anticipate of life in a land beyond the horizon, the realities of an 8 to 3 bell schedule and the daily regimen of lesson plans, student discipline, hall duty, and all the rest are much the same whether the school is in Maracaibo or Milwaukee." Joseph S. Kennedy, Director of the American School in Milan, Italy, cautions: "The job is not easier. Parents are very concerned about the education of their children and, as a result, are frequently quite demanding." Parents of children in international schools are concerned that their children's education will compare favorably with stateside schools so that they will be prepared to reenter American schools as transfer students or college freshmen without academic difficulty. This concern, and the fact that the school is usually the focal point of the American community, often require that teachers and administrators devote extra time to assist parents and students with transitions between the United States and the host country or vice versa.

Educators who have not been successful in finding a suitable position in the United States may think of overseas employment as a way of increasing their chances of entering or reentering the profession. Since the early 1970s, competition for jobs in United States schools and colleges has been intense, and the number of qualified applicants has often dramatically exceeded the number of available positions. While it is possible to expand one's options by considering foreign opportunities, applying to international schools must not be considered a means of escaping from the competitive job market in the United States or a remedy for the problem of unemployment. Like most American schools, overseas schools are usually able to select from a large pool of well-qualified professionals.

SEEKING FRIENDSHIP OR ROMANCE

Obviously, accepting a position overseas assures that an educator will meet a variety of new people upon relocation. It is certainly true that lasting friendships and even romance may develop in the course of a foreign assignment; however, it is important to recognize that such relationships are no more likely to occur abroad than at home. Educators who go abroad with the expectation of expanding social contacts or finding the ideal marital partner may be severely disappointed. Bruce R. Fehn, currently teaching in Thessaloniki, Greece, comments on the potential for loneliness, "especially if you are single and live in a country where English is not typically spoken. Making friends in a highly different cultural setting can be a slow process. Most overseas schools follow the norm for schools in the United States—they are staffed by teachers who are married. They are not enclaves of swinging, single expatriates."

The nature of the relationships formed among faculty members abroad is necessarily different from typical relationships among those in United States schools. As guests in a foreign country, faculty members are likely to be more dependent upon each other for both professional and social needs. Language barriers and housing arrangements may tend to draw members of the American community into closely knit groups. The sharing of experiences often extends beyond the school environment; it is not uncommon for educators to spend much of their leisure time together and even to travel together during school holidays and vacations. The closeness and intensity of the relationships create a bonding that frequently endures beyond the term of the assignment. As Thomas H. Mohr, a veteran overseas teacher, reflects: "The friendships developed in an overseas environment last for a lifetime. There is something about similar goals and interests that draws people together."

Regardless of how a particular foreign environment may encourage—or set limits on—the development of friendships or romantic relationships, educators need to realize that most people are very much the same whether they are working in Des Moines or Dacca. Those who make friends easily at home are likely to make friends easily abroad—at least within the American community. Conversely, a person who chooses to spend leisure time alone in the United States will probably elect the same life-style overseas. Either type of individual can find an overseas experience both fulfilling and rewarding, but the educator should not expect the new location to alter or to transform the ability to develop and maintain satisfying personal relationships.

MAKING MONEY

Although educators usually do not expect their profession to make them wealthy, C. Patrick Hotle, who has experience in Central America and North Africa, claims that as an international educator, he "can live the life of a jet-setter without having the money." Most experienced educators view their foreign experiences as personally and professionally, though not necessarily financially, rewarding. International schools generally offer adequate but not lavish compensation, although salaries may vary widely depending upon location. Currently, Americans working abroad may receive $75,000 in earned income before the salary is subject to taxation by the Internal Revenue Service. In order for this tax break to apply, an educator must be out of the United States for 330 days of any twelve consecutive months. In some situations, particularly if salaries are exempt from both U.S. and host-country income taxes, educators may earn a considerably higher net income than in comparable stateside positions. However, even in the most lucrative situations, living expenses and the cost of recreation and sight-seeing may account for a significant portion of the earnings. Most educators can expect their standard of living in a foreign country to be equivalent to or higher than what they have been accustomed to in the United States, but people going abroad for the first time may be surprised or even shocked at the price of automobiles, gasoline, housing, food, and personal services.

Employers and experienced teachers alike warn against the idea of going overseas to accumulate savings or to overcome financial difficulties. Touring within the host country, taking holiday trips to other nations, entertaining friends, and shopping for souvenirs or specialty items unique to the location are an integral part of the international adventure and should not be passed up in order to save a few dollars. Depending upon individual circumstances, it may be possible to conclude an overseas assignment with a financial gain, but any such result should be considered a pleasant bonus and should not be anticipated, nor should it be a major consideration in the decision to pursue overseas employment.

PREREQUISITES FOR SUCCESS

However strong the motivation to seek an international career may be, the desire to live and work abroad must be assessed realistically. Overseas living is not for everyone; some people should limit their international experiences to brief jaunts or package tours. Before expending the time, effort, and money required for a job search that may prove to be both lengthy and expensive, educators must determine whether they have the requisite characteristics to succeed in an assignment thousands of miles from home. Foremost among these characteristics are independence, good health, and flexibility.

Educators who are overly dependent upon the comforts, conveniences, and familiar surroundings of home are likely to be disappointed and frustrated abroad. Similarly, football fanatics, fast-food junkies, or TV addicts may be happier indulging their pleasures at home in Dubuque or Tallahassee than experiencing withdrawal symptoms in Lusaka or Lucerne. Individuals with unusually strong ties to family or friends may find lengthy separation difficult, especially if relatives and friends remaining in the United States have not wholeheartedly accepted and supported the educator's decision to go abroad. It is natural for family and friends to feel a sense of loss at the educator's departure, but if the move to a foreign country is perceived as abandonment or escape, the educator is far more likely to experience anxiety, stress, and guilt. Such responses will greatly interfere with the educator's ability to cope with the adjustments and accommodations necessitated by an overseas relocation.

Personal health must be a consideration for anyone planning to go abroad for extended periods of time. Adverse physical reactions to extremes of climate or elevation may not preclude the possibility of living overseas but may place restrictions or limitations on the job search. Certainly, individuals with chronic health problems requiring constant attention would be well advised to remain in locations where medical services are readily available; for some, this may mean remaining in the United States.

The third prerequisite for a successful foreign experience, flexibility, was specifically mentioned by nearly every teacher and administrator who contributed advice and suggestions for this book. Being flexible means having the ability to adapt to existing situations, to perceive and appreciate cultural differences, and to maintain a sense of humor. Without flexibility, discomfort and unhappiness are virtually inevitable. Merritt B. Jensen, Headmaster of Japan's Nagoya International School, aptly describes key elements in this basic ingredient for success: "Be tolerant of different cultures and customs. Plan to leave your American customs at home and melt into the host country as quickly as possible." Melting into the host country, as Jensen recommends, does not mean that American values must be abandoned, nor does it mean that Americans living abroad must disappear inconspicuously into the society of the host country. Flexibility involves living compatibly with another culture, recognizing and accepting cultural differences, and understanding that "the American way" is not the only way.

Independent, healthy, flexible educators who believe they are willing and able to adapt to a foreign setting generally find they can point to several good reasons for seeking employment abroad. Whatever the initial motivations may have been, when these educators return home they nearly always find they have experienced multiple rewards. Kathleen L. Johns, a principal in Lisbon, Portugal, touches on the feelings expressed by many overseas educators about the rewards of their experience: "A successful overseas teaching experience gives one the realization that there is a world outside of the United States. One gains the concept of internationalism which is lacking in people who understand only nationalism. One sees firsthand the interaction of world politics and economics. Of course, there is also the wide opportunity for travel, for seeing beautiful historical and natural sights, for meeting people of other nationalities, and for gaining the broad background necessary to good teaching."

Decide on the area of the world in which you wish to teach. Find names of schools in that area through directories. Contact them directly or find a recruiting fair near you.

Thomas H. Mohr
Tripoli, Libya

I received information regarding my present position from my placement office, with follow-up interviews at the AAIE (Association for the Advancement of International Education) convention. In addition, I interviewed at a college recruiting fair.

James Braunger
Taipei, Taiwan

Be flexible and willing to take less than desired if your real interest is in going abroad. It is often easier to move once overseas than to come fresh from the States.

R. L. Ater
Brussels, Belgium

I feel it is important not to be too restrictive about the locations you would be willing to go to. Write to several schools to inquire about opportunities. There are publications available that list the schools and give quite good descriptions of each.

Floyd L. Hall
La Paz, Bolivia

Chapter Two

Starting the Job Search

After considering motivations for working abroad and deciding to seek a new position in a foreign country, educators need to begin transforming pleasant daydreams into concrete realities. Overseas positions cannot be rushed into, nor should they be casually sought. The decision to pursue international employment involves a commitment of time, energy, and money. Whatever the educator's background and previous experience, time and resources must be budgeted for research, evaluation, organization, and the development and effective use of appropriate job-seeking skills and strategies. The overseas job search may be a long and arduous process; designing and implementing a successful job campaign can take from six months to a year—or even longer. The search will, however, be an exciting period of professional stimulation and personal discovery.

The procedures for finding a suitable position overseas are neither a secret nor a mystery, nor are desirable positions discovered only in an international version of the infamous "hidden job market." A large and well-defined market exists for educators of all types—teachers, administrators, librarians, counselors, and other auxiliary personnel. Becoming familiar with the various options available in international education is a logical and important first step in the employment process. This chapter will introduce both primary and secondary sources of information about educational opportunities, discuss personal and professional priorities, and outline specific procedures for starting a job search. The options presented are not to be considered exhaustive, but they will serve as a starting point for individual investigation of educational career opportunities outside the United States.

EMPLOYMENT OPTIONS

In every part of the world where Americans are living and working, schools have been established to provide educational opportunities for children of U.S. citizens and for others seeking American-style educational programs. These schools offer a curriculum similar to a typical elementary or secondary school in the United States, so that in the event of transfer to another overseas location or back to the United States, students can continue their education with minimal academic adjustment. Depending upon location, schools may be independent American-sponsored schools, company-sponsored schools, independent private schools, or U.S. military-sponsored schools. College professors may consider working for overseas branches of American colleges and universities or in private or public foreign universities. In addition, opportunities for educators exist in international exchange programs, in language schools, in nonprofit organizations, and in religious and voluntary services. In the following section are presented brief, general descriptions of the various types of overseas employment opportunities for educators and sources of information about each.

ELEMENTARY AND SECONDARY SCHOOL OPPORTUNITIES

American-Sponsored Overseas Schools

In approximately ninety countries, American citizens have established independent, nonsectarian, coeducational schools. The U.S. government does not operate or control these private schools, but the schools receive or have at some time received financial assistance from the U.S. Department of State. Each school is governed by a board of education elected by the parents of children enrolled in the school. Teachers and administrators are recruited from many different countries, including the host country, but most are Americans or American-trained. The board of education establishes a salary schedule, and compensation varies depending upon the size of the school, the location, and the cost of living in the community. Salaries may be subject to taxation by the host country. The principal source of each school's operating budget is derived from tuition payments and gifts from corporations and individuals. Many corporations employing U.S. citizens will pay the tuition for dependent children attending these American-sponsored schools.

Facilities and enrollments vary greatly from country to country. For example, some schools are located on embassy grounds, others in apartment buildings in the center of the city, and still others on large, multibuilding suburban campuses. The student body is often multinational and multilingual, including children of American citizens as well as children from the host country and other countries. The curriculum is very similar to that found in a typical school in the United States, and the language of instruction is English.

Detailed descriptions of American-sponsored schools, including information about organization, curriculum, faculty, enrollment, and facilities, are available in the form of fact sheets prepared by the Office of Overseas Schools. Libraries and college placement offices may have copies of these fact sheets, or information can be obtained from:

Director
Office of Overseas Schools
U.S. Department of State
Washington, D.C. 20520.

Company-Sponsored Schools

Some large American businesses and corporations operate private schools for the children of their employees stationed abroad. These schools vary in size depending upon the location and the population served. The schools are governed by a board of trustees and employ certified teachers from the United States to implement a curriculum comparable to that of U.S. public schools. All instruction is in English. Depending upon the company and the location of the school, housing, furnishings, and transportation may be provided for staff members. Salaries reflect the cost of living in the host country and range from adequate to excellent. Host-country taxes may be levied, but some corporations offer a bonus to employees to defray tax expenses.

Other Private Schools

In addition to the American-sponsored and company-sponsored schools, a number of other independent boarding or day schools for English-speaking students exist overseas. These schools have been established by private citizens of the host country, citizens of the United States or other countries residing in the community, religious organizations, or other special-interest groups. Both American teachers and host-country nationals may be recruited as staff members. Parent-sponsored schools are typically governed by a board of directors representing parents of children enrolled in the schools as well as other elements of the community. Compensation schedules vary depending upon location and other factors, and as in American-sponsored and company-sponsored schools, salaries may be subject to host-country taxes.

Information about these three types of independent international schools can be found in the directories listed below, which provide data on the name and type of school, address, academic head, staff size, student enrollment, tuition, facilities and physical setting, nature of program, and academic calendar. College placement offices or academic libraries generally contain one or more of the following publications:

Directory of the European Council of International Schools, published by the European Council of International Schools, Inc., 19 Claremont Road, Surbiton, Surrey KT6 4QR, England;

ISS Directory of Overseas Schools, published by International Schools Services, Inc., P.O. Box 5910, Princeton, New Jersey 08540;

Peterson's Annual Guide to Independent Secondary Schools, published by Peterson's Guides, Inc., P.O. Box 2123, Princeton, New Jersey 08540;

Schools Abroad of Interest to Americans, published by Porter Sargent Publications, Inc., 11 Beacon Street, Boston, Massachusetts 02108.

Department of Defense Dependents Schools

The Department of Defense sponsors and funds elementary and secondary schools for the dependents of military and civilian personnel serving on overseas bases situated in more than twenty countries. School size and facilities vary considerably from country to country, and students represent diverse cultural and educational backgrounds. The curriculum is patterned after public schools in the United States and is taught and administered by certified teachers and supervisory personnel from the United States. Generally, salaries are comparable to those offered in stateside urban areas, and contracts include similar benefits. Tax breaks applicable to Americans working abroad do not apply to employees of the Department of Defense Dependents Schools. Salaries are subject to U.S. income tax and, where applicable, state income tax from the educator's home state.

Educators applying for positions in Department of Defense Dependents Schools must agree to be available for worldwide placement; however, applicants may express a preference for any of the following six regions:

ATLANTIC REGION	MEDITERRANEAN REGION
Belgium	Azores
Bermuda	Bahrain
British West Indies (Antigua)	Greece
Canada (Newfoundland)	Italy
Cuba	Spain
England	Turkey
Iceland	
Netherlands	PACIFIC REGION
Norway	Japan
Scotland	Korea
	Okinawa (Japan)
GERMANY (NORTH REGION)	Philippines
GERMANY (SOUTH REGION)	PANAMA REGION

The Department of Defense transports educators and their dependents as well as household goods and other personal possessions to and from the duty station. If military housing is not available, a living quarters allowance is provided. Applicants for positions in the Department of Defense Dependents Schools are considered on the basis of several requirements. Applicants must have had at least one year of professional experience in education within the past five years. (This experience must have been at the grade level or in the subject field for which the applicant wishes to be considered.) Elementary teachers must be willing to teach at any level within the primary or intermediate grades; secondary school teachers must be certified and willing to teach in more than one area. Interest in coaching or sponsoring other extracurricular activities is advantageous if not absolutely required. Applicants must be U.S. citizens and are required to have a bachelor's degree, 18 semester hours of college courses in teacher education, and a valid teaching certificate or credential issued by a state department of public instruction or state-approved college or university.

For additional information, contact:

> Department of Defense Dependents Schools
> Teacher Recruitment Section
> Hoffman Building I
> 2461 Eisenhower Avenue
> Alexandria, Virginia 22331.

United States Department of Education

Educators have the opportunity to participate in exchange programs between the United States and other countries. Teachers, school administrators, and curriculum specialists can gain firsthand experience of another country and its culture by actually working in a foreign educational system. International exchange programs and summer sessions are administered by the U.S. Department of Education under the auspices of the Mutual Educational and Cultural Exchange (Fulbright-Hays) Act of 1961.

Teacher Exchanges. Although specific arrangements may vary depending upon the country, most educators taking part in teacher exchange programs are employed through a direct exchange with their foreign counterparts. The American teacher and the foreign teacher exchange classroom responsibilities and, in some cases, may independently arrange to exchange houses or apartments, cars, and even pets. Exchange educators are thoroughly screened and must be recommended by the Fulbright Commission and local authorities. Foreign teachers must be approved by local school officials in the United States before the exchange can be effected.

American teachers who wish to participate in the exchange program must have U.S. citizenship, have at least a bachelor's degree, be currently employed in a full-time teaching assignment, and have at least three years of professional experience in the appropriate subject field and/or grade level. In addition, they must receive approval for the exchange from their local school administration, which normally will grant the participating educator a leave of absence for the duration of the exchange program. Although teaching couples may apply, opportunities for joint appointments in a direct exchange are extremely limited. Teaching couples may be considered for separate placements if they so indicate. Salaries for exchange teachers are determined by the administrators of the participating schools. Compensation is based on the teacher's training and experience and the local salary schedule and is paid in the currency of the host country. Salaries of American teachers are subject to U.S. income tax. Transportation for the teacher may be fully or partially funded; dependents may accompany the educator, but a transportation allowance for dependents is not provided.

Summer Seminars. Educators at all levels, from elementary teachers through college professors, can be considered for participation in summer seminars conducted in various parts of the world. Information about scheduled seminars that is made available by the Department of Education includes the location, type of seminar and sponsor, dates, eligibility requirements, itinerary, program content, number of participants, terms of award, and allowances for transportation or other expenses. The minimum requirement for participation is two to three years of successful teaching experience and current employment in a position relevant to the topic of the seminar. Housing allowances, if provided, are paid in the currency of the host country and are based on the local cost of living. Seminar participants should be prepared to cover all personal expenses and generally may not be accompanied by dependents. Applications must be submitted before November 1 for participation in the following summer's programs.

For complete information about Teacher Exchange Programs and Summer Seminars, contact:

Teacher Exchange Branch
Division of International Services and Improvement
International Education Programs
U.S. Department of Education
Washington, D.C. 20202.

OPPORTUNITIES IN HIGHER EDUCATION

University of Maryland University College

In cooperation with the United States Department of Defense, the University of Maryland offers credit programs of undergraduate study for armed services personnel and members of federal agencies who are stationed abroad. American educators are needed to staff these programs, which exist in the European

Division (Azores, Belgium, Greece, Iceland, Italy, the Netherlands, Portugal, Spain, Turkey, United Kingdom, and West Germany) and in the Asian Division (Guam, Japan, the Philippines, and South Korea). Courses are offered in the disciplines of Anthropology, Business and Management, Computer Science, Criminology, Economics, English, Government and Politics, History, Law Enforcement, Philosophy, Science, Sociology, and Speech.

One-year appointments as Lecturers (renewable to a maximum of four years) are available to educators who hold a doctoral degree or, in some fields, to those who have completed all requirements for the doctorate except the dissertation. Educators who are qualified to teach in more than one academic discipline are preferred. Requirements include U.S. citizenship, recent college-level teaching experience, and evidence of excellence in teaching. Faculty members are required to relocate within the Division in which they are employed after one or two terms. Four 8-week terms constitute an academic year.

Salaries are based on academic credentials and experience, although they generally do not exceed salaries for lower-division instructors in stateside colleges. Transportation from the United States to the overseas post is furnished. Health insurance and retirement plans are available, and in most locations, benefits also include access to military post exchanges and commissaries. Housing is not provided for faculty members, nor are special allowances for dependents offered.

For complete information, applicants are encouraged to send a vita and letter of interest to:

Assistant to the Chancellor/Overseas Programs
University of Maryland University College
University Boulevard at Adelphi Road
College Park, Maryland 20742.

Foreign Universities

Teaching and research opportunities for academics can be found in public and private universities around the world. Foreign universities routinely recruit faculty members from the United States for both temporary and permanent appointments. Positions may be advertised through placement offices or agencies; in professional journals; or in newspapers such as the *Chronicle of Higher Education,* the *New York Times,* and the *London Times Higher Education Supplement.* Educators interested in positions in Africa and the Middle East may contact the following organizations for information about job listings:

The African-American Institute
833 United Nations Plaza
New York, New York 10017

America-Mideast Educational & Training Services
1717 Massachusetts Avenue, N.W., Suite 100
Washington, D.C. 20036.

Educators are sometimes hired for fixed-term assignments through private United States foundations. Those receiving appointments may serve as faculty members in a foreign institution or as staff members of the sponsoring foundation. Among the major foundations offering overseas appointments are the following:

Carnegie Corporation of New York
437 Madison Avenue
New York, New York 10022

The Ford Foundation
320 East 43rd Street
New York, New York 10017

Charles F. Kettering Foundation
5335 Far Hills Avenue
Dayton, Ohio 45429

The Rockefeller Foundation
1133 Avenue of the Americas
New York, New York 10036.

A useful publication for educators considering overseas opportunities in college-level teaching or related areas is *Careers in International Affairs,* published by Georgetown University's School of Foreign Service. Most academic libraries will contain one or more of the following directories, which will provide information about specific academic programs and may be used as a starting point for direct contact with institutions of interest.

Commonwealth Universities Yearbook
Covers colleges and universities in the British Commonwealth. Lists faculty and administrators, degrees offered, enrollment, library facilities, and special programs.

International Handbook of Education Systems
Covers education systems in Europe and Canada, Africa and the Middle East, and Asia, Australia, and Latin America. In addition to specific

educational data, includes information about each country's geography, population, society and culture, history and politics, and economy.

International Handbook of Universities
Covers 5,000 colleges and universities in more than 100 countries. Includes names of administrators and department heads, school history, academic calendar, language of instruction, international exchange programs, and library volumes.

World Guide to Universities
Covers more than 5,600 universities and colleges worldwide that grant doctoral degrees and offer postdoctoral studies. Includes names of administrators and faculty, courses offered, and student enrollment.

World List of Universities
Lists approximately 6,000 universities and other institutions of higher education in 151 countries. Also includes international and regional organizations and associations concerned with higher education.

The World of Learning
Covers 24,000 universities, colleges, research institutes, libraries, and scientific, educational, and cultural organizations and learned societies around the world. Includes names and addresses of principal officers and titles of periodic publications.

(For complete publication information about the volumes described above, see INFORMATION SOURCES FOR OVERSEAS OPPORTUNITIES in Appendix I.)

Educators currently studying or employed in colleges or universities in the United States often can obtain useful information from campus offices for international education and from faculty members and graduate students who have engaged in overseas teaching or research. In addition, many colleges have cooperative programs with foreign institutions whereby undergraduate students may spend a semester or year abroad. Such programs may provide educators with a direct link to potential employers.

Fulbright Programs

Advanced graduate students who have completed all requirements for the doctoral degree except the dissertation may be eligible for a Fulbright grant under the Doctoral Dissertation Research Abroad Program. Applicants must be completing a degree in a modern foreign language or an area studies program, have a suitable research project, and possess sufficient language skills to carry out that project. Grants are not awarded to applicants with research projects that focus on Western European nations or on countries with which the United States does not maintain diplomatic relations. The applicant must be a citizen or permanent resident of the United States and must be planning to pursue a career in higher education.

The Fulbright Senior Scholar Program offers opportunities for teaching and/or research at institutions of higher learning in various locations in Africa, Australia and New Zealand, Central and South America, Eastern Europe and the U.S.S.R., East and Southeast Asia, the Middle East and North Africa, South Asia, and Western Europe. While some regional awards are available, most grants are awarded for teaching or research within a single country and generally extend for the entire academic year of the host institution. Grants for shorter periods are also available in some countries.

Lectureships and research awards are offered in a wide range of academic disciplines, including the following:

Agriculture	Food Technology and Nutrition
American Studies	Geography
Archaeology and Anthropology	History
Architecture and Urban Planning	Language and Literature
Art and Art History	Law
Biological Sciences	Library and Information Science
Business and Management	Linguistics
Chemistry	Mathematics and Statistics
Communications and Journalism	Medical Sciences and Services
Computer Science	Music and Theater
Earth and Atmospheric Sciences	Philosophy and Religion
Ecology and Environment	Physics
Economics	Political Science and Public Administration
Education	Psychology
Engineering and Technology	Sociology and Social Work
English as a Foreign Language	

Applicants for Fulbright Senior Scholar grants must be U.S. citizens. Lecturers are usually required to have postdoctoral teaching experience in the field (and at the appropriate level) for which the lectureship is sought. Although a doctoral degree is required for most appointments, teachers of English to speakers of other languages may be eligible with a master's degree, and lectureships in the creative arts do not require advanced degrees. Applicants for research awards are expected to have completed the doctorate (or other terminal degree) at the time of application. Applicants for either a lectureship or research award may, in some cases, be required to be proficient in a foreign language. Eligibility for the awards is restricted to people who have not lived abroad for the ten years preceding their application. Preference is given to applicants who have had little or no overseas experience.

Benefits vary depending on the type of grant received, duration of appointment, and location. Most grants include allowances for travel, living expenses, and incidental costs for the educator and accompanying dependents. All Fulbright grants are subject to U.S. taxes.

For complete information about these and other grants, educators currently working or studying at graduate institutions in the United States are encouraged to contact the office of the graduate dean, the office of sponsored programs, or the office of international programs on their campuses. Educators employed at four-year colleges and community colleges should consult with their chief academic officer. Information may also be obtained by contacting:

> Council for International Exchange of Scholars
> Eleven Dupont Circle, Suite 300
> Washington, D.C. 20036.

In cooperation with the Fulbright programs, the International Research and Exchanges Board (IREX) provides scholars at the advanced graduate student and postdoctoral levels with the opportunity to conduct research abroad for periods of up to ten months. IREX concentrates on exchange programs with countries in Eastern Europe and the U.S.S.R. Applicants must be U.S. citizens, proficient in the language of the host country, and affiliated with a North American college or university. Further information is available from:

> International Research and Exchanges Board
> 655 Third Avenue
> New York, New York 10017.

OPPORTUNITIES WITH INTERNATIONAL ORGANIZATIONS

Many international organizations sponsor and maintain educational programs in countries throughout the world. The majority of these opportunities are likely to be in Third World developing countries. Some educators may be hired as short-term staff and given assignments of a few months' duration. Church mission-related organizations may offer contracts requiring long-term commitments of at least four years with possibilities for renewal. Although positions with some organizations include full salaries, others—particularly in service or religious organizations—provide staff members with only a small stipend or subsistence allowance.

United Nations

An agency of the United Nations of special interest to educators seeking employment overseas is the United Nations Educational, Scientific, and Cultural Organization (UNESCO). The UNESCO Technical Assistance Program recruits U.S. citizens for a limited number of field posts in the UNESCO programs for developing countries. Specialists are needed in teacher education, curriculum development, science education, educational innovation, technology, and media. Applicants must have a doctoral degree and a minimum of five years of experience in higher education. For complete information, inquiries should be directed to:

> UNESCO Recruitment
> Division of International Education
> U.S. Department of Education
> Washington, D.C. 20202-6103.

Other United Nations divisions with international employment possibilities for educators include the United Nations Children's Fund (UNICEF), World Health Organization (WHO), Food and Agriculture Organization (FAO), and United Nations Development Program (UNDP). Information about opportunities within these United Nations divisions may be obtained from:

> Recruitment Programmes Section
> Division of Recruitment
> Office of Personnel Services
> United Nations
> New York, New York 10017.

Peace Corps

Almost everyone is familiar with the Peace Corps, but many people do not realize that more than one-third of its volunteers are engaged in teaching. A Peace Corps appointment usually lasts two years; it may involve teaching in an urban setting or in a remote village. Assignments vary in the nature of the responsibilities and duties, and proficiency in the language of the host country may be required. Before departure, Peace Corps volunteers participate in a stateside orientation session, and upon arrival in their host country they typically receive three months of additional training. When necessary, intensive language study forms part of the training. Although Peace Corps workers are called volunteers, they are paid a nominal salary, which is usually sufficient for daily living in the host country. In addition, for each month of service, the Peace Corps sets aside a certain amount of money that will be paid to volunteers upon their completion of the assignment and return to the United States. Additional information and application forms may be obtained from regional ACTION Recruiting Centers or from:

> ACTION
> 806 Connecticut Avenue, N.W.
> Washington, D.C. 20525.

YMCA Overseas Service Corps

The Overseas Service Corps of the YMCA is a service organization offering teaching opportunities in Japan and Taiwan. Applicants must be native speakers of English and recent college graduates. A background in linguistics or in the teaching of English as a foreign language is desirable, although teaching certification is not required. Knowledge of Japanese or Chinese is helpful but not required; however, applicants should demonstrate some background or interest in Japanese, Chinese, or Asian studies. Responsibilities may vary from classroom instruction and curriculum development to extracurricular activities or participation in language camps. Students represent a variety of backgrounds and occupations and may range from teenagers to adults of all ages. Assignments are for an initial term of two years in Japan or one year in Taiwan. Benefits include salary and a housing allowance (which varies with the size of the city to which the educator is assigned) and full or partial transportation allowances. For complete information, contact:

> YMCA of the U.S.A.
> Overseas Service Corps
> International Division
> 101 North Wacker Drive
> Chicago, Illinois 60606.

Other Opportunities

Educators at all levels may find many opportunities for volunteer or paid services with a variety of other international organizations as well as with independent development agencies, United States government agencies, and church missions. An excellent source of information about such organizations, with descriptions of their programs and functions and addresses for direct contact, is *The Overseas List,* by David M. Beckmann and Elizabeth Anne Donnelly. Another useful publication for information about nonprofit organizations is *Careers in International Affairs,* published by the School of Foreign Service of Georgetown University.

ESTABLISHING PRIORITIES

The information in the preceding pages is intended to help educators interested in international job opportunities to launch an in-depth investigation of the options available to them. Such an investigation will involve several stages and varying amounts of time, possibly spread over several weeks or even months. The scope of the research will be determined by the educator's interest in and need to obtain either general information about overseas teaching or specific information about a particular region, country, community, or individual school. In the course of conducting this research, educators will find it helpful to establish basic priorities. At the beginning of an overseas job search it may seem difficult or even impossible to think of developing a list of priorities, but such a list will help the educator to identify or confirm motivations for seeking an international employment experience—and perhaps to focus energies on a particular geographic region. The outcome of a carefully considered list of priorities may also be the discovery—often unexpected by first-time job seekers—that going abroad is the priority, and that location, type of school, or exact assignment is of secondary importance.

For the educator whose top priority is to experience another culture, the advice from experienced professionals is especially relevant. Michael Robinson, Director of the Cochabamba Cooperative School in Bolivia, says: "Be flexible and adaptable and willing to work anywhere for your first job." Gary Goodell, a teacher in Brussels, Belgium, advises teachers to "be willing to take a less desirable job at first in order to get your foot in the door."

With this advice in mind, educators should carefully consider the following factors in developing a list of priorities that reflects both personal and professional goals and interests:

- *Region*
  Travel opportunities
  Climate
  Political stability
  Cultural differences

- *Country*
  Political base
  Stability of government and economy
  Currency rate and exchange
  Language
  Religion and toleration of differences

- *Community*
  Housing
  Cultural and leisure activities
  Location and size
  Accessibility and transportation
  Standard of living
  Health services
  Spouse activities and opportunities
  Children's accommodations and education
  Media (newspapers, books, TV, radio)

- *Professional*
  Salary/benefits
  Philosophy
  Private school atmosphere
  Curriculum and number of class preparations
  Resources (media, lab equipment, curriculum materials)
  Student/teacher ratio
  Facilities (buildings and grounds)

Developing a priorities list is beneficial to educators at all stages in their career. Veteran overseas educators and hopeful first-time applicants alike will gain from first giving some serious thought to priorities and then proceeding to gather relevant information. Locating appropriate materials may involve trips to the library to find books about the country or countries of special interest in order to become familiar with cultural, economic, and political considerations. Foreign embassies, consulates, or cultural centers offer another good source of information. (For addresses of these and related sources of information, see Appendix II.) College and university placement offices or international education centers might also be consulted. It may even be possible to identify people within the community who have worked in the region of interest and who can offer firsthand impressions.

THE NEXT STEP

Determining the types of educational settings of interest, becoming familiar with the resources available for acquiring information about specific opportunities in overseas schools or universities, and establishing a set of priorities are essential preliminary steps in the process of securing an international job. The specific procedures and resources used will depend upon the type of position sought, the academic degrees and teaching or administrative certificates held, and the amount of experience accumulated. Once the preliminary research has been done, however, there is no one way or best way to proceed in order to obtain employment overseas; educators have located positions abroad by their own efforts or by using an intermediate placement office or employment agency.

PLACEMENT SERVICES

College placement offices and independent employment agencies offer services that educators may find instrumental not only as a source of information about overseas opportunities but also as a means of conveying academic and professional records to potential employers. Some educators routinely use the services of both college placement offices and independent agencies to assist them in their job search.

College Placement Offices

Educators at all levels, from elementary through postsecondary, often begin the job search by contacting a college placement office for information and resources. In addition to establishing or updating a placement file containing the educator's credentials and references, the placement office may be able to provide much specific information about the overseas job market. Some international schools and foreign universities list vacancies with campus placement offices. Resource centers may contain international directories and related materials. Placement advisers may have firsthand knowledge of international institutions or may know alumni who are currently working abroad or have returned from overseas positions. Advisers may also assist in the preparation of résumés and vitae designed specifically for overseas employment. Job seekers should check with their college placement office to determine the availability of services and resources.

Employment Agencies

A small number of independent agencies specialize in providing placement abroad for teachers and administrators in international schools and for college and university professors and researchers. Individual agencies have varying requirements for registration; some require that educators have a minimum of two years of recent teaching or administrative experience, have a personal interview with an agency representative, establish an agency placement file, and pay a registration fee. Costs vary according to the services offered and often will include a placement fee if the applicant secures a position through the services of the agency. Placement fees may be a flat rate or may be based upon a percentage of the educator's first-year salary. Before entering into an agreement with an agency, it is important to ask these five basic questions:

What types of positions are handled by the agency? (level, location, etc.)

How often are vacancies reported to registrants?

How many vacancies can I expect to hear of?

How long will my registration materials be kept active?

What fees will be required?

While all of these questions need to be addressed, it is especially important to understand the exact nature of the financial commitment in order to avoid unexpected expenses and needless resentment once a position has been secured. In some cases, the employer may pay all or a portion of the agency's placement fee, but this practice is by no means universal. If the fee is the job seeker's responsibility, arrangements for payment (lump sum on acceptance of position, deferred payment, etc.) should be clearly understood in advance.

Elementary and secondary school teachers and administrators may wish to contact the following agencies for complete information about their services:

> European Council of International Schools
> 19 Claremont Road
> Surbiton, Surrey KT6 4QR, England

> International Schools Services
> 126 Alexander Street, P.O. Box 5910
> Princeton, New Jersey 08540

> Overseas Schools Services
> 446 Louise Street
> Farmville, Virginia 23901.

Individuals seeking college and university positions in foreign countries may wish to become familiar with the Register for International Service in Education (RISE). RISE is a computer-based referral system administered by the Institute of International Education. The referral service has been designed to match college and university teachers, researchers, specialists, consultants, and technician-trainers who have been educated in the United States with opportunities in foreign countries. RISE assists universities, professional schools, technical institutes, research centers, government ministries, and other agencies in locating qualified professionals for long-term and short-term assignments. Although primarily designed to help developing countries find educators and specialists, the service is available to educational institutions and related agencies or projects in all countries. It accepts registrants in a broad range of fields, including the arts and humanities, the social, physical, and life sciences, education, mathematics, business, health, agriculture, engineering, and other technical and professional areas. RISE collects biographical data from individual registrants and makes this information available to prospective employers. The data assembled includes academic discipline, specialization, degree(s) earned, dissertation or thesis topic, career experience, language competencies, publications, and references. A small registration fee is required of individuals, but there is no placement fee. For complete information about this postsecondary referral agency, educators should contact:

> Director
> RISE
> Institute of International Education
> 809 United Nations Plaza
> New York, New York 10017.

CONFERENCES AND RECRUITING FAIRS

Administrators of elementary and secondary schools from around the world attend the annual stateside conference of the Association for the Advancement of International Education, typically held in the latter half of February. According to Gordon E. Parsons, Executive Director of the Association: "AAIE's goals are to provide the overseas schools with an annual conference that is designed to keep the school current on recent trends in American education, and to provide in-service training workshops for overseas administrators and teachers." Administrators attending the annual conference of the AAIE often schedule interviews with applicants for teaching and administrative positions on an informal basis. The Association provides interview space and a bulletin board display of job announcements and candidate résumés. Information about the annual conferences and the Association's monthly publication, *Inter-Ed,* can be obtained from:

> Association for the Advancement of International Education
> Room 200, Norman Hall
> College of Education
> University of Florida
> Gainesville, Florida 32611.

Other conferences primarily of interest to teachers and administrators already employed in overseas schools are sponsored by the European Council of

International Schools. The November conference, held in various cities in Europe, is intended for all elementary and secondary educators, and a spring conference is usually attended by administrators. The purpose of the conferences is to promote professional growth and development among international educators, but the conferences also provide opportunities for recruitment and interviewing. Information can be obtained from:

European Council of International Schools
18 Lavant Street
Petersfield, Hampshire GU32 3EW, England.

Representatives of elementary- and secondary-level international schools frequently attend recruiting fairs sponsored by independent agencies or college placement offices. Although these fairs differ in size and scope, some weekend fairs make it possible for administrators from dozens of international schools to interview hundreds of certified teachers and administrators. Employers and applicants alike find that recruiting fairs provide maximum interview opportunities in a minimum amount of time. The agency or placement office sponsoring the fair establishes requirements for participation. Typical registration requirements include a minimum of two years of recent teaching or administrative experience, submission of current professional references, and payment of a fee. College-sponsored fairs are usually established on a nonprofit basis; fairs sponsored by independent agencies are typically profit-making ventures. In recent years, overseas recruiting fairs have been held in the following cities:

CEDAR FALLS, IOWA
Midwest Overseas Recruiting Fair
152 Gilchrist Hall
Education Center
University of Northern Iowa
Cedar Falls, Iowa 50614

CLEVELAND, OHIO
Teacher Overseas Recruitment Center
National Teacher Placement Bureau
P.O. Box 9027
Cleveland, Ohio 44109

LOS ANGELES, CALIFORNIA
California Overseas Teaching Interviews

Placement and Career Planning Center
University of California at Los Angeles
Los Angeles, California 90024

NEW YORK, NEW YORK, and ATHENS, GREECE
International Recruitment Center
International Schools Services
P.O. Box 5910
Princeton, New Jersey 08540

LONDON, ENGLAND
ECIS Recruitment Centre
European Council of International Schools
18 Lavant Street
Petersfield, Hampshire GU32 3EW, England.

Recruiting fairs may sometimes be held on other college campuses as well. College placement offices can provide information about dates and locations. Because most fairs are conducted in February and March, inquiries regarding the fairs should be made in the preceding fall.

PERSONAL CONTACTS AND NETWORKS

Many professionals have found international positions through personal contacts. At the beginning of a job search educators may feel that this avenue is not open to them because they simply don't know anyone who has lived or taught overseas. This need not be an obstacle, however; once educators begin telling people of their interest in pursuing a career abroad, they will find that contacts gradually develop. This approach may sound simplistic, but it is almost always effective. Efforts need not be concentrated only on colleagues—job seekers should talk to everyone. Sooner or later, a connection will be made with someone who has knowledge of a specific overseas location or even a specific international school. Finding useful contacts is not accomplished overnight; it is a slow process that may take several months, but it is a beginning. Once a few contacts or links have been established, it is possible to develop a network of people who may be useful in providing information, impressions, and even an inside track to finding a suitable position abroad.

Once a contact has been established, a job seeker can then request permission to use that person's name in communications with prospective employers. Philip G. Houseal, a former teacher in Ilo, Peru, suggests that "the best way to get overseas is through someone who has taught or worked at the school you are interested in. Administrators overseas are very particular about their teachers . . . they prefer to hire someone they know or know about." A personal recommendation by an educator who is currently located overseas or who has had recent experience abroad is indeed a valuable one.

Stating the name of a personal contact in a letter of introduction or inquiry sets the letter apart from several, perhaps hundreds, of unsolicited letters and usually assures that it will capture the administrator's interest. A letter of inquiry often serves as the initial point of contact between the job seeker and prospective employer; this very important document will be discussed and illustrated in the following chapter.

Contacts will continue to play an important role throughout a person's professional career. Joseph S. Kennedy, Headmaster of the American School of Milan, states that he learned of his current position in Italy through the "grapevine" that exists in the overseas schools. It is, in fact, quite common for experienced educators who are a part of the overseas circuit to learn of openings in various other locations through friends and colleagues. Developing a network of contacts can be extremely effective in any job search provided that the individual contacts, when sought for referral purposes, are used wisely. It is important to realize that however useful a network may be in the overseas employment process, it can sometimes work against a job seeker if any one contact is less than dependable, capable, or respected.

GAMBLING OR INVESTING?

Although any of the approaches described above for finding a position abroad can be used individually, each educator's circumstances will determine the method or combination of methods that will be most effective. The educator's employment objective, geographic preferences, present location, and the time of year the search is begun are all factors that will influence the nature and direction of an overseas employment search. Whether the educator seeks jobs through a college placement office or a private employment agency or chooses to attend conferences and recruitment fairs, starting the search will demand a personal investment of both time and money. There are no guarantees; exploring new possibilities in any field of endeavor always involves an element of risk. Educators who are duly qualified, persistent, and well prepared minimize the risks of disappointment. The application procedures and interviewing techniques outlined in the next two chapters will help educators to master the paperwork and personal skills necessary to maximize their chances for success.

A résumé should include as much information as possible in order for it to act on your behalf and in your absence. It is a tool that should be used to arouse interest.

Thomas J. Rushcamp
Jeddah, Saudi Arabia

Give exactly what is requested; keep everything brief and to the point. Needless to say, everything should be clearly marked, well organized, and neat.

Milt Pavlina
São Paulo, Brazil

Both letters and résumés should be well organized and brief. Every attempt should be made to organize in outline style so that as much information as possible is stated but stated concisely. Narratives do not get much attention. An administrator wants an "at-a-glance" overview. NEVER should correspondence be written longhand. Well-organized business letters and professionally printed résumés get top attention. It shows that the candidate has respect for himself and for the institution to which he is applying.

Kathleen L. Johns
Lisbon, Portugal

Interest in possible employment should be initiated by the candidates through a brief letter accompanied by a short résumé listing educational background, certification, prior experience, and position desired. Letter and résumé should be well written and neatly prepared. Since each overseas school has its own application format and procedures, the candidate should be prepared to complete all documentation and steps immediately upon receiving a positive response from a school.

Curtis C. Harvey
Cali, Colombia

Chapter Three

Preparing the Paperwork

In the early stages of the search for a teaching or administrative position abroad, the résumé or vita—with an accompanying cover letter of application or inquiry—forms a crucial link between job applicants and their potential employers. Later, the official application form may play a significant role in the applicant's final evaluation against any number of competing job seekers. In order that these introductory documents receive full consideration, it is essential that they convey clearly and precisely the applicant's qualifications and interests. Merritt B. Jensen, Headmaster at Nagoya International School in Nagoya, Japan, offers the following advice to educators seeking overseas employment: "Put your best foot forward. Sell yourself. Be succinct. Be honest. Be candid." This chapter is designed to help educators prepare the primary kinds of paperwork—résumés and vitae, cover letters, and application forms—that will serve as essential tools in the application process.

In approaching the application process, most people think of the letter of application or inquiry as the first task to be considered, and it is true that this letter is usually the first communication to which the employer's attention is directed. Because the initial contact with an employer generally will consist of both a cover letter and a résumé or vita, it is essential to consider these documents as a package. Before the cover letter can be written, however, it is necessary for the job seeker to develop and draw upon information in the résumé or vita that will accompany it. Constructing an effective résumé is the foundation of any job search and should precede any other writing task applicants will undertake.

RÉSUMÉS AND VITAE

As a means of introduction to prospective employers, every educator needs a document briefly describing academic background and professional experiences. This document may be either a résumé or a vita, depending upon the applicant's background and job objective. A vita (also known as a curriculum vitae, or c.v.) is a form of résumé used primarily for employment in higher education. It is distinguished by its detailed emphasis on educational background and academic achievement. Job seekers with advanced degrees who are pursuing college-level positions abroad will, in most cases, need to prepare a vita; certified teachers and administrators seeking positions in elementary and secondary schools typically prepare a résumé. The terms *résumé* and *vita* will be used respectively in this chapter when distinctions are pertinent. For comments applicable to either document, the term *résumé* will be used alone.

A résumé used for pursuing overseas employment opportunities will differ from the typical résumé used in a stateside job campaign. It must be tailored specifically for overseas positions and in this respect should be considered a single-purpose document. Items that would not be emphasized or perhaps even mentioned in a résumé for positions in the United States may be important and necessary elements of the overseas résumé. For example, information about citizenship and family status may be required by overseas school boards or hiring officials in order for them to consider an applicant for a staff position. The following capsulized list and accompanying notes on résumé dos and don'ts should be studied carefully before résumé preparation is begun.

DO

Include full name, complete address, and telephone number

Provide complete information about educational background and certification

List all professional experience

Volunteer relevant personal data

Emphasize travel or study abroad

Inform the reader of language competencies

Indicate possibilities for extracurricular assignments

State availability of credentials or references

Create a professional image

Organize material logically

DON'T

Include outdated or irrelevant information

Mislead, exaggerate, or lie

Exceed reasonable space limits

Mention salary

34

Identification

The résumé should contain the applicant's complete name, address, and telephone number. A permanent forwarding address should be included, if appropriate. To eliminate confusion, avoid abbreviations and spell out all parts of the address in full.

Educational Background

It is essential to state degrees earned or in progress and the name of the institution or institutions attended. Academic honors may be included in this section (e.g., B.A. cum laude). The title or topic of the thesis or dissertation may also be included, along with names of academic advisers or principal teachers for M.A. or Ph.D. candidates or degree holders. Location and date of high school graduation are optional inclusions, although any attendance at an overseas school, whether in the elementary or secondary grades or in college, should be listed.

Certification

Certification areas should be stated specifically and completely so that an employer can determine at a glance what the applicant is licensed to teach or direct. Areas of emphasis as well as any temporary certification should also be included. Some international schools may consider assigning their teachers to two or even three teaching areas. A clear statement of certification areas generally will eliminate the need for including a "Position Desired" or "Career Objective" section on the overseas résumé.

Professional Experience

Identify professional experiences in education by title of position, location, and dates of employment, preferably in reverse chronological order. Concise descriptions of current and previous experiences should be provided. Job seekers with advanced degrees should include research and teaching assistantships in this section. The résumé will be most effective if experiences are described in strong, action-oriented words (e.g., *initiated, organized, motivated, developed*). If gaps have occurred between professional experiences, create a category to include other kinds of work experiences (e.g., Insurance Representative, XYZ Company), with inclusive dates. Educators with limited professional experience may describe student teaching assignments, especially if such inclusions demonstrate additional subject competencies or experience at different grade levels. Details of previous extracurricular responsibilities, such as athletic or drama coaching, yearbook or newspaper advising, or student government sponsorship, are also appropriate inclusions in this section.

Teaching/Research Interests

A separate statement of specific teaching or research interests can serve to emphasize the breadth of one's academic background or one's qualifications in special areas. Certificated teachers may want to mention several general teaching areas (e.g., social studies, English, French). Applicants with graduate degrees may choose to indicate specific courses they are prepared to teach.

Publications/Presentations/Professional Activities

Papers presented at professional conferences or published in scholarly journals should be cited, along with book reviews, workshop participation and leadership, or other professional activities. Nonscholarly publications may also be included, if appropriate. Certificated teachers and administrators should list any involvement with curriculum writing or the preparation of student handbooks. Memberships or offices held in professional organizations are also appropriate items for inclusion.

Travel or Study Abroad

Include dates and locations of any foreign travel or study undertaken as an undergraduate or graduate student. Evidence that an applicant has gained cultural awareness through living, studying, or traveling abroad is important. Prospective employers will be favorably impressed by applicants who have already demonstrated the interest and ability to experience and explore another culture. They are likely to recognize the value of the experience even though it may have taken place in a different part of the world from the location of their school. A relatively inexperienced educator with extensive travel experience or experience as a foreign exchange student could receive special consideration.

Language Competencies

As with travel experience, any knowledge of a foreign language can be an advantage and should be cited—regardless of whether the language included is that of the host country and regardless of the degree of proficiency. Although applicants should not claim greater ability than they in fact possess, competencies should always be presented positively; for example, to describe a limited reading knowledge of a language, merely stating "Some reading ability" is sufficient and far preferable to the negative phrase "Poor reading ability."

Extracurricular Possibilities

Extracurricular activities are an integral part of most primary- and secondary-level international schools, and any professional experience in this area should be stated on the résumé. In many international schools a large proportion of the faculty is expected to take an active part in coaching sports or sponsoring extracurricular activities of various kinds. Applicants who do not have previous experience with extracurricular duties but who feel qualified to supervise or assist in such activities should indicate their interest in doing so. Mentioning past participation in college or community theater, student government, athletic programs, or comparable activities may also help.

Personal Data

Applicants should include data on citizenship, marital status, number of children and their ages, and spouse's occupation. Except in the case of schools directly operated by the U.S. government, educational institutions overseas may not be bound by regulations that prohibit employers from requesting of job applicants certain types of personal information, such as marital or family status. Because of the unique situation of many international schools and colleges, such information may be considered essential by hiring personnel and therefore should be provided voluntarily by the applicant. A recent notice from Stavanger American School in Norway illustrates the kind of restrictions that may exist in some overseas positions: "Because of the acute shortage of suitable housing in Norway (resulting from the North Sea oil exploration), applicants may be single or married but with not more than one child. Teachers with more than one child need not apply. Teaching couples may be considered, but the possibility of suitable vacancies for both is not very good."

The age of dependents can be a significant factor in consideration for employment, especially if the employing school provides education only at elementary and junior high school levels. In this case, dependents who are secondary school students might have to attend boarding schools in other locations or else return to the United States for their high school education. Listing the spouse's occupation may be useful in the event that work opportunities are available in other sectors of the community. Joseph S. Kennedy, Superintendent at the American School of Milan, Italy, suggests that applicants "make certain that the interviewer understands the family situation clearly—married, divorced, number of children, etc. Certain questions sometimes cannot be asked, but the administrator must have sufficient information in order to make plans for the teacher."

References and Credentials

Employers will require several references from current and previous administrators or supervisors. In addition, the applicant's principal instructors or academic advisers may serve as useful references. Information about references must appear on the résumé in one of three ways. The educator may indicate that references are available upon request; or, if credentials (including references) are currently on file with a college placement office or a private placement service, the applicant may provide the complete name, address, and telephone number of the placement office. Alternatively, the names, addresses, and telephone numbers of individual references may be listed on the résumé itself. Before submitting the name of a reference, an applicant should always obtain the person's permission to do so. It is important that potential references be informed of the job seeker's intentions and also be given adequate time to prepare the recommendation.

Professional Image

The content and appearance of the résumé combine either to enhance or to detract from the professional image of the educator. One of the first considerations must be the selection and arrangement of information. The layout should be determined by the amount of material to be included and the priority assigned to each item. Just as the items included speak for the applicant, so does the language used to convey the information. Word choice must be correct, easily understood, and sufficiently varied to avoid monotonous repetition or redundancy. Categories of the résumé must be clearly identified with exact and effective designations. Without exception, the tone of the résumé must convey a positive impression by stressing the educator's strengths and achievements. Applicants must be aware that however admirable the content of the résumé, the image will be totally destroyed by incorrect grammar, spelling errors, or a less than perfect physical presentation.

Because of the expense of airmail postage, it is advantageous to select lightweight paper for the overseas résumé. Professional printers may be able to offer helpful suggestions regarding layout and design and the choice of high-quality, lightweight paper. Whether the finished product is typed or professionally printed, the copy must be free of typographical errors. This requires careful proofreading—and is probably best accomplished when more than one person checks the final copy. If the résumé is to be professionally typeset, the printer's proof must be carefully checked before the production run is made.

Outdated or Irrelevant Information

Educators with many years of experience must be especially aware that a comprehensive listing of every activity is rarely necessary or even appropriate for the overseas résumé. Committee assignments, religious and community activities, and summer or part-time employment should be thoroughly evaluated in terms of current relevance and listed sparingly, if at all. If such information is to be included, it should be selective and representative rather than exhaustive.

Accuracy and Honesty

Applicants should never attempt to misrepresent their credentials or achievements. Academic and professional information contained on the overseas résumé may be subjected to verification by prospective employers. Hiring officials frequently do check with previous employers, and the discovery of any discrepancy will automatically eliminate an applicant from further consideration. As Donald L. Ballentine, Associate Superintendent of the Dhahran International School in Saudi Arabia, warns, "Don't con me." This advice is reinforced by Headmaster Richard F. Underwood, of the Seoul Foreign School in Korea, who states, "By all means, be 100% honest. Any job you get by deception will be a disaster far greater than the 'disaster' of not being hired."

Reasonable Limits

If the résumé has been prepared properly, length should not be a problem. Conciseness is desirable, and a one-page résumé is often quite effective. Although restricting the résumé to a single page is not always possible, it will not be to an applicant's advantage to exceed two pages. It is never permissible to use both sides of the page; if two pages are required, they must be typed or printed on separate sheets, with the applicant's full name appearing at the top of the second page.

Salary

Salaries for most positions in international educational institutions are largely determined by schedule. Because of cost-of-living variables, varying tax situations, and other potentially significant factors such as housing allowances, salaries are not always easily compared to those paid in American schools and colleges. The résumé is definitely not the place to discuss salary history, requirements, or expectations. Financial considerations are appropriately discussed only in later stages of the application process.

SAMPLE RÉSUMÉS AND VITAE

On the following pages are four sample résumés and two vitae. They represent applicants with different career objectives and different levels of experience and educational background, ranging from bachelor's degree holders to candidates with doctoral degrees. The samples illustrate a variety of possible formats, category designations, and phrasing options suitable for the overseas résumé; each is followed by a detailed explanation of how and why particular choices serve to present the applicant's qualifications to best advantage. A thorough study of all of the samples should be undertaken before résumé construction is begun.

STEPHEN NAGEL

P.O. Box 721
Bismarck, North Dakota 58501
(701) 777-2700

U.S. Citizenship
Married
Teaching Spouse

―――――――――――――TEACHING EXPERIENCE―――――――――――――

1970 - 1972	Seaford Elementary School, Seaford, Delaware. 3rd grade traditional, self-contained classroom.
1972 - 1978	Westwinds Alternative Elementary School, Dade County System, Miami, Florida. 2nd grade, team teaching, open-space classroom.
1978 - present	Custer Elementary School, Bismarck, North Dakota. 4th and 5th grade combination classroom.

―――――――――――――COACHING EXPERIENCE―――――――――――――

1975 - 1978	YMCA boys' basketball club coach, Miami.
1979 - 1981	Summer baseball coach, Bismarck.
	Qualified to coach all boys' and girls' sports.

―――――――――――――CERTIFICATION―――――――――――――

North Dakota (K-9)   Delaware (K-8)   Florida Permanent (K-8)

―――――――――――――FAMILY INFORMATION―――――――――――――

Jane Nagel (wife), B.A., Delaware State College, 1969. Elementary teacher with art endorsement, 6 years' teaching experience.

Two daughters, ages 8 years and 4 years.

―――――――――――――EDUCATION―――――――――――――

1966 - 1970	Delaware State College B.S., Elementary Education	Dover, Delaware
1975 - 1977 Summer Sessions	University of Miami Reading endorsement	Coral Gables, Florida

―――――――――――――REFERENCES AVAILABLE UPON REQUEST―――――――――――――

The sample résumé of Stephen Nagel is very basic and has been designed to accompany a general letter of inquiry. Material is presented without detailed description, but all essential categories are represented and are arranged in order of strength. Stephen has included with other personal data the fact that his wife is a teacher, because he knows that some international schools prefer to hire teaching couples. His teaching experiences have been presented in chronological order. For consistency, other categories also follow this pattern. Without going into great detail, Stephen has given the employer a clear picture of the grade levels and the types of classroom setting in which he has taught. Dates have been set off at the left in order to emphasize the number of years of experience he has gained as his career has progressed. Coaching ability and experience have been highlighted by creating a separate category for this information. The CERTIFICATION category contains two important pieces of information: (1) Stephen is licensed to teach in three states; (2) Stephen is qualified to teach at the elementary, middle school, and junior high levels.

The FAMILY INFORMATION category emphasizes the academic background and experience of Stephen's wife but does not present details of her experience. If Jane were to apply for employment, her résumé would be submitted individually. The number of children and their ages are listed because these can be important factors for prospective employers, who must consider housing and educational opportunities for dependents of the teaching staff.

Stephen's educational training is not recent, nor does he hold an advanced degree. Placing the EDUCATION category near the end of the résumé gives it less prominence and serves to focus attention instead on Stephen's major strength, the amount and scope of his teaching experience. The statement REFERENCES ARE AVAILABLE UPON REQUEST indicates that supporting recommendations will be furnished at the appropriate stage of the selection process. When accompanying an initial letter of inquiry, as this résumé is intended to do, it is not essential that the résumé list the names of references or indicate the placement office or agency from which references can be obtained.

JOANNE L. JAMES

439 Iowa Avenue
Blue Earth, Minnesota 56013
(507) 526-4836

EDUCATIONAL BACKGROUND:

English Education	Master of Arts	1981
University of Wisconsin	Madison, Wisconsin	
English/History	Bachelor of Science	1979
Ripon College	Ripon, Wisconsin	

PROFESSIONAL EXPERIENCE:

English instructor, 1981 - present, Blue Earth High School, Blue Earth, Minnesota. Teaching responsibilities include: sophomore general English, junior level American Authors Survey Course, and an honors seminar on contemporary literature. Developed curriculum for honors seminar, designed learning centers in general English, and assisted with textbook selection for the authors course.

STUDENT TEACHING:

English and American history student teacher, spring semester, 1979, Ripon Junior High School, Ripon, Wisconsin. Taught three sections of 7th grade basic English and one section of 8th grade American History. Designed tests and evaluated student progress, participated in open house, and organized field trips to the Milwaukee Early Colonial Museum. Throughout the semester, worked with lecture groups, small seminars, and individual students.

TRAVEL ABROAD:

Co-sponsored State of Wisconsin Student Tour Group	
Federal Republic of Germany	Summer 1981
Toured Southern Europe & North Africa	May–August 1978
AFS Student Brussels, Belguim	Junior Year 1975

LANGUAGE ABILITIES:

French - conversationally fluent, read and write
Spanish - read

```
                                                    JOANNE L. JAMES
                                                          -2-



PROFESSIONAL        Phi Delta Kappa
AFFILIATIONS:       Minnesota Education Association
                    National Council of Teachers of English




COLLEGE             Graduated with highest honors, Ripon College      1979
HONORS:             Awarded the President's Young Scholar Certificate  1979




SPECIAL             Traveling, photography, gourmet cooking, classical music,
INTERESTS:          tennis, stamp collecting.




CITIZENSHIP &       U.S.A.
MARITAL STATUS:     Single, no dependents




CREDENTIALS         Educational Placement and Career Services
AVAILABLE:          B150 Education Building
                    1000 Bascom Mall
                    University of Wisconsin-Madison
                    Madison, Wisconsin 53706
                    (608) 262-1755
```

Like the résumé of Stephen Nagel, Joanne James's résumé (see pages 42–43) could be used with a general letter of inquiry. Given its greater detail, it could also accompany a letter of application for a particular opening or serve as an introduction to an interview. Because she has an advanced degree, Joanne has chosen to begin her résumé with the category EDUCATIONAL BACKGROUND. In addition to describing her current employment under PROFESSIONAL EXPERIENCE, she gives a capsule description of her work as a student teacher. There are three reasons for doing this: (1) her professional experience is limited; (2) her student teaching was at a different level than her subsequent employment; (3) the experience included an assignment in a second teaching field.

Joanne purposely has arranged her two-page résumé so that the TRAVEL ABROAD and LANGUAGE ABILITIES categories would appear on the first page. Her travel and living experiences abroad are definite assets that will help to offset her limited professional experience.

Joanne has chosen a format that emphasizes categories rather than years or dates. The blocks of information are easy to read because they are surrounded by ample areas of white space. The applicant's full name is repeated on the second page alongside the page number.

The PROFESSIONAL AFFILIATIONS category shows that Joanne is active in professional associations. COLLEGE HONORS indicates her high scholastic ability, which may be of particular interest to some employers. Including SPECIAL INTERESTS helps to define the applicant as a well-rounded individual. As on all résumés intended for an international job search, Joanne's résumé clearly states her citizenship and marital status.

Even though Joanne will arrange to send a copy of her placement file to her prospective employer, she has included the complete name and address of her college placement office under CREDENTIALS AVAILABLE. Because credentials can be misplaced during a hectic recruitment schedule—or lost in the mail—the address may save the employer a great deal of time should a second set of credentials be required.

VERONICA R. GEORGE ▄▄▄▄▄▄▄▄▄▄▄▄▄▄▄▄▄▄▄▄▄▄▄▄

Addresses: 14 Airway Drive   Mesa USD #4
            Tempe, Arizona 85283   Mesa, Arizona 85203
            (602) 839-2212 (home)   (647) 112-1001 (office)

PROFESSIONAL BACKGROUND

Administration:
Middle School Principal, Carson Middle School, Mesa, Arizona, 1981 – present.
    Responsible for administration of a staff of 28 teachers; bilingual/
    multicultural student body of 420.

Assistant Principal, McClintock High School, Tempe, Arizona, 1979 – 1981.
    Duties included discipline, attendance, behavioral conferences
    and class and staff scheduling.

Counseling/Teaching:
Head Counselor, Grand River Academy, Austinburg, Ohio, 1975 – 1978.

Counselor/Family Living Teacher, 1972 – 1975, and Home Economics Teacher,
    1969 – 1971, Grant Junior High School, Portsmouth, Ohio.

ACADEMIC TRAINING

University of Arizona   1978 – 1979   Ed.S.   Educational Administration
Tucson, Arizona   1971 – 1972   M.A.   Counseling

Marian College   1965 – 1969   B.S.   Home Economics &
Indianapolis, Indiana   Family Studies

PUBLICATIONS

"Discipline in Decline," The Executive Educator, November 1981.
"Counseling the College Bound Student," Psychology Today, March 1977.

PROFESSIONAL MEMBERSHIPS

American School Counselors Association
National Association of Secondary School Principals
University of Arizona Committee for Friends of Foreign Students

LANGUAGE & TRAVEL

Bilingual – Spanish/English
Traveled extensively in the continental U.S.A. & Mexico.

PERSONAL DATA

Born in Wisconsin; married to freelance writer/photographer, no dependents.

REFERENCES

Peter Jones, Superintendent, Mesa USD #4 (647) 213-7904
Joseph Paul, Principal, McClintock High School (647) 112-7654
Rhea Adams, Director, Grand River Academy (419) 671-4646
Denise Schultz, Dean, College of Education, University of Arizona
    (602) 887-8765

Veronica George's résumé on the preceding page begins with a summary of her professional experiences, which she has divided into two functional categories (<u>Administration</u> and <u>Counseling/Teaching</u>) to facilitate scanning. Since employers are generally most interested in the applicant's recent work, professional experiences have been arranged in reverse chronological order, and this order has been used in all categories throughout the résumé. Veronica's description of her current position gives basic information about the size and type of school for which she is responsible. Because the duties of an assistant principal are usually less clearly defined, she has delineated her specific duties in the description of her previous administrative position.

Education has been given second place in the arrangement of the résumé. Although her degrees and educational background are good, Veronica feels that her varied professional experience represents her major strength as an applicant. The categories of PUBLICATIONS and PROFESSIONAL MEMBERSHIPS demonstrate her expertise in her field as well as her commitment to professional involvement.

The LANGUAGE AND TRAVEL information included in the résumé indicates Veronica's interest in another culture and emphasizes the fact that she is bilingual. The use of the term *bilingual* tells the employer that the applicant has complete mastery of the second language.

Like Stephen Nagel and Joanne James, Veronica has indicated her marital status under PERSONAL DATA. Rather than simply omitting any mention of children, the statement "no dependents" unmistakably informs the reader that no children will accompany the applicant.

It should be noted that the option of listing references on the résumé is not recommended as a standard procedure and should be used only if the applicant does not make use of the services of a placement office or agency. Veronica has included the names and addresses of references on her résumé because she has not yet established a file with a placement service. She has, of course, contacted the people she has listed and obtained permission to give their names to prospective employers.

MICHAEL P. TAKIS

51 Glendale Road
Taft, California 93268
(734) 545-7890 home
(734) 432-5543 office

Desire position as Overseas School Chief Administrator or Director

ACADEMIC TRAINING

Ph.D.	Claremont Graduate School Claremont, California	1976	Education Administration
M.A.	University of Washington Seattle, Washington	1968	Secondary Curriculum and Administration
B.S.	Seattle University Seattle, Washington	1962	Math & Philosophy

EXPERIENCE SUMMARY

Superintendent	six years
High School Principal	three years
High School Assistant Principal	three years
Secondary Teacher	six years

AREAS OF EXPERTISE

Curriculum Development	Budget
Inservice Training	Negotiations
Community Relations	Staffing

ADMINISTRATIVE BACKGROUND

Superintendent, 1979 - present   Taft Union High School District, Taft,
California. High school enrollment of 980, instructional staff of 60,
non-teaching staff of 25. Sixty-eight percent of seniors attend postsecondary institutions.

Superintendent, 1976 - 1979   Westwood Unified District, Westwood,
California. School district enrollment of 480.

High School Principal, 1971 - 1974   Yreka Union High School District, Yreka,
California. School system enrollment of 1,000.

Assistant High School Principal, 1968 - 1971   North Beach School District
#64, Copalis Beach, Washington. School system enrollment of 760.

TAKIS
-2-

TEACHING EXPERIENCE

Secondary math teacher and drama sponsor, 1964 - 1967, The Frankfurt International School, Frankfurt, Germany.

Secondary math teacher, 1962 - 1964, Grand Coulee Dam School District, Coulee Dam, Washington.

TRAVEL & LANGUAGES

Traveled extensively in Germany, Poland, Yugoslavia, and Bulgaria. Speak fluent German and can read French and Latin.

CIVIC & PROFESSIONAL ACTIVITIES

Board Chairman	Taft United Way	1980 - present
Vice President	Westwood Conservation Project	1977 - 1979
Actor & Director	Community Theatre	1965 - present

Executive board Member	CEPA	1981 - present
(California Educational Placement Association)		
Member	AASA	1976 - present
(American Association of School Administrators)		
Member & past officer	Phi Delta Kappa	1968 - present

PERSONAL INFORMATION

Married, wife is former Public Health Nurse   1 son, sophomore at Stanford

PLACEMENT FILE

Placement and Career Planning, Claremont Graduate School, 131 McManus, Claremont, California 91711   (714) 621-8177 ext. 374

The résumé prepared by Michael Takis immediately identifies the type of administrative position he is seeking. If an overseas job applicant wishes to include on the résumé a statement about the professional or job objective, the statement must focus on a particular position or type of position. More than one résumé should be prepared if the applicant is seeking more than one type of job. The statement must reflect the applicant's immediate job choice; references to long-range plans are not appropriate on an overseas résumé.

Because the doctorate is an asset for the type of position Michael seeks, it has been placed first in the résumé. Immediately following ACADEMIC TRAINING, Michael has provided a brief summary of his professional experience and areas of strength. In this way he directs the employer's attention to his key qualifications. The employer then does not have to abstract relevant information from the more detailed accounts of professional experience that follow.

The sections covering Michael's professional experiences include all relevant names, locations, and dates of employment. School size is stated for each of the administrative experiences, with greater detail about staff size for the most recent position. The majority of students in international schools are college-bound; bearing this in mind, Michael has provided relevant data from his previous assignments.

Although Michael knows that travel experience and language competencies are of interest to prospective employers, he has placed them on the second page of his résumé because he feels, correctly, that they are subordinate to the major strengths represented by his professional experience and academic qualifications.

As an educational leader, Michael realizes the importance of his participation in a variety of civic and cultural responsibilities. Based on his previous teaching experience abroad, he knows that in foreign countries the school very often functions as the center of the American community. The brief and selective list of professional and civic activities has been carefully chosen to demonstrate his ability to work with different types of organizations and with different elements in the community.

The personal information Michael has presented answers any questions a search committee might have about his family status. It indicates that no dependent children will accompany him and also implies that his spouse, though professionally trained, is not currently seeking employment.

EDWARD A. CHARLES

1261 Second Avenue
Gainesville, Florida 32610
(904) 391-2368

ACADEMIC PREPARATION	B.S. - Agronomy, 1977
	Oklahoma State University, Stillwater, Oklahoma
	
	M.S. - Agronomy, 1980
	University of Florida, Gainesville, Florida
	
	Ph.D. - Agronomy (to be completed summer, 1985)
	University of Florida, Gainesville, Florida
	
	    Dissertation topic: Conservation of tropical pastures and
	    forages in the broadlands of western Venezuela

GRADUATE COURSE CONCENTRATION	Pasture Management Agronomic Problems Quantitative & Advanced Genetics Ecosystems of the Tropics Design of Mechanized Systems Agricultural Economics Agronomic Methods of Forage Technical Writing Evaluation

EXPERIENCE SUMMARY	Peace Corps Volunteer, Paranam, Surinam
	    Adviser of local farming cooperative; responsible for
	    planning, developing, and implementing new farming
	    methods relative to proper use of equipment and farming
	    systems. 1977-1979
	
	Agricultural Consultant, University of Zulia, Maracaibo,
	    Venezuela
	    Involved in research and fieldwork with responsibility for
	    providing technical assistance to area farmers; activities
	    included extensive interaction with governmental agencies
	    relative to funding and program developments. 1980-1982
	
	Research Assistant, University of Florida, Gainesville, Florida
	    Assisted Professor David Kanellis with research techniques
	    in the area of tropical forages and pastures; contributed to
	    several articles and papers authored and presented by Dr.
	    Kanellis. 1982-1983
	
	Doctorate Field Study - Venezuela
	    Ford Foundation Foreign Area Fellowship grant for the
	    study of development of agronomic plants in tropical areas
	    to meet the continuing need for increased food supplies.
	    1983-1984

PAPERS PRESENTED	"Fertilization and Grass-growing Techniques for Guinea Grass," presented at 10th Annual Conference on Cattle and Poultry Production in Latin America, Maracaibo, Venezuela. April, 1982 "The Use of Nitrogen in Tropical Pastures," presented at 12th Annual Conference on Cattle and Poultry Production in Latin America, Gainesville, Florida. April, 1984

Page Two

EDWARD A. CHARLES

INSTITUTES AND CONFERENCES ATTENDED	National Council of Agricultural Investigations, Annual Conference, Caracas, Venezuela. July, 1982
	Soils and Crops Science Society of Florida, Annual Conference, Jacksonville, Florida. May, 1983
	Southeast Regional Institute of Soil Conservation, Jackson, Mississippi. September, 1983
HONORS AND MEMBERSHIPS	National Merit Scholar, 1973
	Governor's Award for Agricultural Studies, 1976
	B.S. degree awarded magna cum laude, 1977
	Secretary, Graduate Student Senate, University of Florida, 1982-1983
	Honorary Memberships in Phi Kappa Phi, Alpha Zeta, and Gamma Sigma Delta
	American Society of Agronomists
	Council for Agricultural Science and Technology
	Soil Conservation Society of America
LANGUAGE COMPETENCIES	Speak, read, and write Spanish fluently
	Good reading knowledge of Portuguese
PERSONAL INFORMATION	United States citizen
	No dependents
REFERENCES AVAILABLE ON REQUEST	Career Planning and Placement Office University of Florida Gainesville, Florida 32611

On the preceding two pages, the vita prepared by Edward Charles illustrates a simple but effective graphic device to separate each category of information. The lines not only call attention to the major divisions of the vita but also help to break up the comparatively dense segments of copy into quantities the reader can more easily absorb at a glance.

Because Edward is currently in the process of completing his doctorate, the academic record is presented first. He has chosen to arrange the information in chronological order to show the progression of his studies and work experiences. This is especially appropriate because all of his degrees are in the same subject area, and there are no significant gaps in his progress toward his terminal degree. To demonstrate the breadth of his graduate studies, Edward has included a category entitled GRADUATE COURSE CONCENTRATION. Although many other courses could have been added, he has selected those he thinks will be of direct interest to his potential employers.

Under EXPERIENCE SUMMARY Edward provides concise descriptions of his principal work experiences and responsibilities since his completion of his undergraduate degree. Later, in the cover letter used as an application for a particular position, he will include relevant highlights and specific details of his various positions.

Edward's inclusion of sections on PAPERS PRESENTED and INSTITUTES AND CONFERENCES ATTENDED is appropriate whether he is applying for a teaching or consulting position. In addition to demonstrating his research productivity, the information contained in these sections shows that he is active in the international community of scholars in his field of study. The items included under HONORS AND MEMBERSHIPS further demonstrate his scholastic ability and leadership.

DORIS ANN HANSEN

ADDRESSES

Home: 21 Royal Avenue
Hamilton, New York 13345
(315) 824-2298

Office: 304 State Building
Colgate University
Hamilton, New York 13346
(315) 823-2351

PROFESSIONAL EXPERIENCE

Teaching

Associate Professor of German, Colgate University, Hamilton, New York, 1984-present

Fulbright-Hays Visiting Lecturer, Department of Germanic Languages and Linguistics, University of Mannheim, Mannheim, Germany, 1983-1984

Assistant Professor of German, Colgate University, Hamilton, New York, 1979-1983

Teaching Assistant, German, The University of Iowa, Iowa City, Iowa, 1977-1979

Instructor, German Language Laboratory, University of Kansas, Lawrence, Kansas, 1976-1977

Related

Translator/Reader for English-language edition of *German Language and Literature Monographs,* 1980-present

Translator of technical writing, Electronics International, Dallas, Texas, 1973-1974

Volunteer

Instructor of English as a Foreign Language for Hamilton Community Center, Hamilton, New York, 1982

Tutor, non-English-speaking students, The University of Iowa, 1971 and 1977-1979

RECENT PROFESSIONAL CONTRIBUTIONS

Publications

Ausklammerung, or the Debracketing Effect in Modern German Speech, forthcoming book (scheduled for release in 1985 by the Harvard University Press, Cambridge, Massachusetts)

"Intonation Cues to Management in Natural Conversation," *Language Behavior Research Laboratory Working Paper Series No. 52,* University of California - Berkeley, Berkeley, California, 1983

Conference Presentations

"Teaching in a Second Language: The Communicative Competence of Non-native-speaking Teaching Assistants," address at Mid-America Linguistics Conference, University of Nebraska, Lincoln, Nebraska, February, 1984

"Word Order in the Older Germanic Dialects," address at Modern Language Association Annual Conference, San Francisco, California, December, 1982

"The Image of the School in Contemporary German Literature," American Association for German Studies Conference, Boston, Massachusetts, April, 1982

Complete list of publications and presentations available upon request.

PROFESSIONAL STUDIES

Stateside

German, Ph.D., 1979. The University of Iowa, Iowa City, Iowa
Dissertation title: A Generative Phonology of Modern Literary German

Linguistics, M.A., 1976. Syracuse University, Syracuse, New York
Thesis title: Levels of Error in Compositions of EFL Students

German and Linguistics, B.A., 1973. The University of Iowa, Iowa City, Iowa

Overseas

Research in contemporary German literature and linguistics, The University of Stuttgart, Stuttgart, Germany, 1978

Germanic studies, Junior Year Abroad Program, The University of Salzburg, Salzburg, Austria, 1971-1972

DORIS ANN HANSEN
Page Two

MEMBERSHIPS

Linguistic Association of Canada and the U.S.
Linguistic Society of America
Modern Language Association
American Association of Teachers of German
Eastern Association for Germanic Studies
Coalition of Women in German
Fulbright Alumni Association
American Association of University Professors

LANGUAGES AND TRAVEL

Excellent knowledge of German, Dutch, and French
Extensive travel in Western Europe, North Africa, and the Mediterranean

CITIZENSHIP

Naturalized United States citizen; born in Flensburg, Germany

RECOMMENDATIONS ON FILE

Educational Placement Office, The University of Iowa, Iowa City, Iowa 52242

Doris Ann Hansen, an experienced college professor, has designed a vita to emphasize both her solid work experience and her numerous professional accomplishments. In presenting her employment history she has omitted detailed descriptions of duties in order to conserve space and because the logical progression of her career does not need extensive annotation. For ease in reading, Doris has divided her professional experiences into three subcategories: Teaching, Related, and Volunteer.

RECENT PROFESSIONAL CONTRIBUTIONS contains a sampling of Doris's publications and conference presentations. In order to keep the vita at a manageable length, she has included only her most recent writings and professional activities. Should an employer desire a complete listing of all publications and presentations, Doris would supply the information as an addendum to the vita, and a comment to this effect has been included.

Because this vita has been designed specifically for an overseas job search, Doris has divided the PROFESSIONAL STUDIES category into stateside and overseas studies. Thesis and dissertation titles have been included to indicate the specific areas of her expertise. Mentioning the nature of the research in which she was engaged in Stuttgart indicates that her interests and background extend beyond linguistics to literature as well. The information about her overseas research experiences demonstrates that her interest in international study is of long standing. The MEMBERSHIPS listings further underscore Doris's commitment to and active participation in her professional field.

The final brief categories of Doris's vita provide additional relevant data about her background and experience. She has indicated her knowledge of additional foreign languages and her acquaintance with a wide range of other cultures. Doris has chosen to inform the employer that she is a naturalized U.S. citizen; the fact that she was born in Germany may provide an interesting point of discussion. Although Doris will arrange to have copies of her references forwarded to prospective employers, the address of the institution where they are maintained has been included for the employer's records.

A FINAL NOTE ABOUT RÉSUMÉS AND VITAE

For all its importance, the résumé or vita is only one part of the application process. At subsequent stages, other documents submitted in support of the candidate's application will be carefully studied by the employing official or search committee. Nevertheless, it is crucial that the reader be able to refer back to the résumé quickly in order to gain, at a glance, any desired information. An innovative presentation may be an asset but is by no means essential. Providing relevant data in a clear, organized, professional manner is more important than attempting to impress the reader with a unique format and design.

Résumés and vitae are needed in a variety of preemployment situations. They may be presented in person to prospective employers while applicants are at recruiting fairs or in other interview situations. Most commonly, however, they are used to establish initial contact with an employer in connection with a letter of inquiry or application. The following section addresses the role of the second basic paper tool, the cover letter.

COVER LETTERS

Letters of application or inquiry that accompany résumés sent to prospective employers are frequently called cover letters. This rather innocuous term can easily be misunderstood. The effective cover letter does a great deal more than simply present the résumé. It serves as an equal partner with the résumé in creating a professional image.

The introductory cover letter—like the résumé it accompanies—is an extremely important element in the successful job search. Employers are looking for people who can communicate clearly and concisely. The cover letter will illustrate the applicant's ability to write clear, complete sentences and to organize information into logical and cohesive paragraphs. Everyone knows that letters must be mechanically perfect and free of misspellings or errors in grammar or punctuation, but it is worth repeating—again and again and again. A single misspelling in a cover letter may prejudice the employer against the applicant even to the extent of removing the applicant from further consideration. A sensible applicant will take the necessary steps to ensure that errors in spelling, grammar, or punctuation do not occur.

Thomas J. Rushcamp, a personnel administrator at the Parents' Cooperative School in Jeddah, Saudi Arabia, brings up another important point about effective cover letters: "Letters of application should be individually typed and personalized. A stenciled form letter is not a good introduction." Regardless of an applicant's ability in penmanship or calligraphy, typed letters are essential. Letters should be typed on the best typewriter available (and if that means renting one, the expense will be justified). The ribbon must be dark and clear and the typeface clean and easy to read; script typefaces are best avoided because they are more appropriate for informal communications and are often difficult to scan. Each letter must be individually typed; photocopies or other mechanical reproductions are never acceptable. Stationery should be of good quality and should match or coordinate with the paper used for the résumé. Lightweight paper and envelopes are preferable because they can make a significant difference in postage expense, but flimsy paper stock should be avoided.

"To whom it may concern" or "Dear Sir" communications are never as effective as letters addressed to the proper individual, and care should be taken to use that person's name and title correctly in the salutation. Avoid making presumptions about title or gender; not all administrators are men, nor do all administrators have a doctoral degree. Names and titles of overseas administrators can, in most cases, be obtained by consulting the appropriate directory of international schools or universities mentioned in Chapter 2.

Letters of Inquiry

The initial letter to a prospective employer may be a letter of inquiry or a letter of application. Letters of inquiry are sent to schools or colleges of interest when the applicant does not know whether openings are available. The purpose of a letter of inquiry is to acquire information about the availability of positions and application procedures. Such letters should be sent very early in the job search, preferably in the fall, soon after the beginning of the school year. The exchange of information that may result from this initial communication can take several weeks or even months and must be accomplished prior to the arrangement of the employer's stateside recruiting schedule. Many letters of inquiry will not be answered, but those that result in a positive reply will require immediate action.

A major feature of a letter of inquiry is the brief overview it provides of the applicant's qualifications. In the sample letter of inquiry on the next page, Paula has attempted to be as general as possible regarding her academic background and experience. At the same time she has tried not to be unnecessarily restrictive about the type of position she would consider. In subsequent communication, should a vacancy occur, she can provide more complete information about specific educational responsibilities and experiences as well as personal qualifications in order to match her background to the available position.

Paula's letter is typed in a standard business format, a modified block style with indented paragraphs. The inside address includes the full name and title of the school administrator, and the administrator's title is used in the salutation. The first paragraph clearly states the purpose of the letter and gives some general introductory information about Paula. A letter of inquiry will have more impact if the reader does not have to spend any time wondering about the purpose of the communication.

The body of Paula's letter refers the reader to the enclosed résumé while highlighting the most significant facts about her previous employment and personal experiences. Because her student teaching assignment was at a different level from her current position, she has included a brief mention of the student teaching in order to demonstrate the breadth of her background. In this way, she increases her chances for possible employment consideration both as a primary teacher and as an experienced intermediate teacher. Paula's travel and living experiences abroad may play an important role in her evaluation against other candidates, so she has used the cover letter to capitalize on her international experience.

SAMPLE LETTER OF INQUIRY

21 Pearl Street
Ottawa, Illinois 61350
October 12, 1983

Timothy J. Stanfield, Ed.D.
Head, Overseas School of Rome
Via Cassia, 811
00189 Rome, Italy

Dear Dr. Stanfield:

Next spring I will complete my third year of teaching in the intermediate grades of the Ottawa Public Schools, and I have decided to pursue a teaching career abroad. The purpose of this letter is to inquire if you anticipate openings in your primary or intermediate program for which I might be considered.

A résumé detailing my educational background and experience is enclosed for your review. Since graduation from the University of Southern Illinois at Carbondale three years ago, I have enjoyed working with the third and fourth graders in my current assignment. As my résumé indicates, my student teaching experience was with a self-contained first-grade classroom, so I feel confident that I can work effectively with students at both primary and intermediate levels.

As the daughter of a retired army officer, I have had the opportunity to travel extensively in the United States and abroad and to experience firsthand the benefits of working and living in other countries. As an elementary student and again in high school I attended Department of Defense schools in Germany and Japan. I enjoy meeting and working with people with varied backgrounds and look forward to working with a multinational student body.

If you anticipate a vacancy, please send an application form and advise me of application procedures. If your plans include a recruiting visit to the United States during the current year, I would be happy to arrange to meet with you to discuss employment opportunities in the Overseas School of Rome.

Sincerely,

Paula Overman

Enc.

SAMPLE LETTER OF APPLICATION

7510 York Drive
St. Louis, Missouri 63120
December 17, 1983

S.B. Arnold, Superintendent
International School of Islamabad
C/o Department of State
Washington, D.C. 20521

Dear Superintendent Arnold:

The Overseas Placement Center has recently notified me of a secondary English vacancy in your school for the coming year. I am very interested in teaching in Pakistan and would like to be considered a serious candidate for your staff opening. The announcement indicated that you will be recruiting at the Midwest Overseas Recruiting Fair in February, which I plan to attend.

I completed my master's degree in English education at the University of South Dakota six years ago. My teaching experiences include two different settings. First, as a junior high English teacher in Dike, Iowa, I taught seventh grade English as well as established and directed a coed intramural program. Four years ago I accepted a position as a high school English teacher in the St. Louis County School System. I have had the opportunity to develop curriculum for existing courses and to create new electives for upperclass students. Teaching in a large urban system, I have worked with students of widely varied academic abilities and ethnic, social, and economic backgrounds. I would welcome the opportunity of living in Islamabad and the challenge of teaching in the International School.

For your review before the recruiting fair, I am enclosing a copy of my résumé and I am requesting that my college placement office send my credentials via air mail. I look forward to hearing from you and to discussing this position in detail with you in February.

Sincerely yours,

Karl Wilken

Enc.

Paula has used her closing paragraph to request information about application procedures as well as the employer's recruiting itinerary. To underscore her availability and interest in interviewing, she ends the letter with a statement expressing her desire for an interview at the employer's convenience.

Letters of Application

In response to an announced vacancy, the applicant prepares a letter of application. In this type of cover letter, the job seeker expresses interest in a specific position, and the focus of the letter should be on those aspects of the applicant's experience and qualifications that relate most closely to the staff opening. In the sample letter on the preceding page, Karl is applying for a position advertised as "secondary English teacher." For this reason, he has included information relevant to both junior- and senior-high levels. The experiences are described in action-oriented phrases, such as "develop curriculum" and "create new electives."

Karl has no foreign language competencies, nor has he traveled abroad, so he has concentrated on his varied teaching experiences, emphasizing the ability to work with students of divergent backgrounds. An important point about this letter is that it stresses the strengths of Karl's background and makes no excuses for his lack of travel experience or foreign language skills. Although the vacancy notice did not mention any specific extracurricular assignments, Karl has volunteered information about previous involvement in an intramural program, which conveys the impression that extracurricular assignments would be welcomed. Karl has also attempted to personalize the letter by using the name of the school and the city where it is located in the body of the letter.

Since the vacancy notice provided only the administrator's initials, Karl has used the salutation "Dear Superintendent Arnold." Another option for the salutation would be "Dear S. B. Arnold." Neither of these alternatives forces the writer to guess at the gender of the employing official. As stated earlier, if gender is not indicated, it should not be assumed. Titles should be used exactly as given. If two titles are indicated, as in "Superintendent S. B. Arnold, Ph.D.," the academic title is preferred, i.e., "Dr. S. B. Arnold."

Karl's opening paragraph accomplishes three distinct purposes. It indicates his interest in the available position, informs the prospective employer that he will be available for an interview at a specific location, and lets the employer know how he learned of the position. Announcements of available positions in international schools may be made through college placement services, overseas placement bulletins, or advertisements in newspapers or journals or by stateside representatives at conferences and recruiting fairs. Although it is not essential, it is a professional courtesy to tell the employer how the writer became aware of the opening. This information will help the employer to evaluate recruiting procedures and advertising effectiveness.

The closing paragraph of the letter again accomplishes three purposes. It refers to the enclosed résumé, expresses Karl's interest in interviewing at the upcoming recruiting fair, and tells the employer that his credentials (contained in his college placement file) are being forwarded in support of the application.

ASSEMBLING A REFERENCE FILE

In any job search, and especially for educators seeking positions in foreign countries, it is important that academic and professional references be assembled and readily available for submission to prospective employers. Each professional experience should be represented by a letter of recommendation from an administrator or department head. Since most employers prefer references written by people in a supervisory position, it is usually neither necessary nor advantageous for elementary and secondary school teachers to ask colleagues to write recommendations. Beginning teachers must have references from their elementary or secondary student teaching assignments; experienced teachers probably have no need for student teaching references unless they are reasonably current or represent an additional teaching field.

Although it is possible to collect and maintain a personal file of letters of recommendation to be submitted to potential employers, most job seekers find it more convenient to establish a file with a college placement office or a private placement agency. Educators who already have a recommendation file in place should consider the current relevance and appropriateness of references that have been assembled for job searches in the past. Employers are most interested in the quality rather than the quantity of recommendations, and outdated or irrelevant references should be deleted from the placement file accordingly. In addition to maintaining current and relevant references, educators should be sure to update academic and professional data contained in the file.

Job seekers may also find it useful to organize a personal file consisting of some or all of the following materials:

- copies of academic and professional data from college or agency placement files
- a list of all references on file and copies of nonconfidential references
- supplemental references (character references, references from university colleagues and students, etc.)
- copies of transcripts, diplomas, and teaching certificates

The personal file can be of assistance at every stage of the overseas job search, especially in the completion of application forms.

APPLICATION FORMS

Typically, the educator's next major task involving paperwork will be the completion of individual application forms. Not all schools use a formal application blank, but many employers consider their application form a key tool in selecting their final pool of candidates. Applicants may receive application forms in response to a cover letter expressing interest in a position, or forms may be provided by a recruiter at an interview. These forms sometimes appear unduly long and detailed, and the applicant faced with completing several different application blanks may find the task repetitive and frustrating. Nevertheless, educators at all levels must treat this screening device as an important and meaningful step in the selection process.

Before attempting to complete the application form, the applicant should read through the entire form to become familiar with the range of information requested. Specific instructions should be followed exactly; for example, a particular section of the form may specify that the response be handwritten. In general, however, most forms will instruct the applicant to type responses. In the absence of specific instructions, a typewriter should be used. The only exception would be if the recruiter requests that the form be completed at the interview site. Whether typed or handwritten, neatness and legibility are critical, and all questions need to be answered fully. If the information requested is not applicable, a dash (—) or the words "Not Applicable" (or its common abbreviated form "N/A") should be typed or written in the space provided. If blanks are not completed, it may appear that the question has been overlooked or deliberately omitted.

Applicants sometimes resent completing application forms because they feel that they have already furnished much of the information requested either on their résumé or through their placement files. Even though the information may be contained in documents that have already been submitted, it is essential to complete the individual application blanks in order to receive full consideration. It is not sufficient to attach a copy of the résumé or to indicate "See résumé" instead of providing a response to specific questions. A thoroughly prepared résumé will make the task of filling out application blanks much easier (and a copy of the résumé should be attached if it has not already been submitted), but it will not serve as a substitute for the completed application form. The employer uses the form as a standard mechanism for collecting uniform data on all applicants. Because the employer is familiar with the format of the application blank, the information required for screening purposes can be obtained quickly and efficiently. If the application blank is incomplete, the employer may look no further.

Personal and Family Information

One of the most striking differences between application forms for foreign employment and most stateside preemployment application forms is the request for information about the applicant's personal history. As noted in the discussion of résumés, items such as date and place of birth, citizenship, marital status, spouse's occupation, number and ages of children, and passport information are often significant factors in the screening process for overseas positions. There are legitimate reasons why international schools may ask these personal questions. Availability of housing and schools for dependents as well as employment opportunities for the applicant's spouse may be very limited or even nonexistent in certain locations. Complete and accurate responses to such questions are therefore essential at this stage of the application process.

Photographs

Applicants often must submit a photograph with the application form. Some forms provide spaces for photos to be attached; others simply ask that a picture be included when the forms are returned. Passport photos generally are the most appropriate in size and often the most convenient to obtain as well. Snapshots should not be used.

Educational Background

Listing institutions attended and degrees earned is a standard part of every application form. Some application forms may request specific information about major and minor areas of study, including the number of hours in the major and minor fields and in education courses (including student teaching). Even if transcripts are submitted along with the application form, the applicant must nevertheless fill in all information requested. Information regarding teaching or administrative certification is also often requested, and applicants should be able to state the type and number of certificates held, date of validity, and subject or level of certificate and state endorsement or approval areas. Some application forms indicate that a copy of the certificate should be attached. The original certificate should never be sent.

Professional Experience

Employers consider it essential to have a formal record of an applicant's employment history. Some application forms will request that only full-time professional experiences be listed; others will also request information about student teaching or graduate assistantships. In addition to basic information such as name of school district, location, employment dates, and title or level of position, applicants may be asked to provide their total years of experience as a teacher or administrator, contract obligations, date of contract expiration, and reasons for desiring a change from their present position. It is important that exact information be provided because employers are likely to request verification of some if not all of the data relating to employment history.

Position Desired

Applicants for teaching positions are usually asked to indicate preferences or priorities in teaching fields and grade levels. On many application forms applicants must indicate first, second, and third choices. If an applicant has no definite preference but is asked to prioritize choices, it is acceptable to indicate a variety of grade levels. For example, an elementary teacher with no particular grade-level preference may simply indicate primary, intermediate, upper level. For those with clear preferences for particular fields or grade levels, it may be helpful to include a brief statement about qualifications and interest in the choices listed.

Extracurricular Activities

Because overseas employers typically expect their teaching staff members to assume extracurricular responsibilities, this topic will usually appear on the application form. Some forms may present a list of extracurricular activities sponsored by the school and request that applicants check any areas in which they could participate as coach or sponsor. Other forms may simply request applicants to list any extracurricular interest, whether it be in coaching sports or in sponsoring student publications, student government, drama, or clubs (chess, photography, etc.). Applicants with strong backgrounds in coaching or sponsoring other activities should capitalize on previous experiences and should be sure to specify the areas in which they are qualified and willing to participate. It is generally advantageous for applicants to express some interest in extracurricular involvement.

Activities, Honors, and Personal Interests

Applicants are often asked to provide information about college or community activities and awards. Employers commonly assume that people with records of involvement and achievement in college and community affairs are more likely to be productive and enthusiastic members of their overseas community. Depending upon available space, applicants may have to be selective rather than exhaustive in their inclusions. Distinctions associated with one's participation should be noted; an applicant who has been an officer in an organization should be sure to include that information and not simply list membership. Variety and range of interests and responsibilities are also important. Employers want to know of personal interests in order to determine if those interests are compatible with opportunities afforded by their location and community.

Languages

Most application forms request information about foreign language competencies. Although the language of instruction in international schools is English, employers are interested in knowing of the applicant's language skills for a variety of reasons. A knowledge of the language of the host country can help ease an employee's adjustment to the new cultural setting. Evidence of knowledge of any language demonstrates an applicant's ability to acquire language skills. Because the student bodies of many international schools are multinational in makeup, an applicant's knowledge of a second or third language may prove useful in assisting foreign students and their families. Applicants usually are asked to identify specific language competencies in three areas: reading, writing, and speaking. As on the résumé, abilities should always be stated positively; for example, one could say, "I have excellent comprehension in German with fair speaking ability." Applicants should avoid negative phrasing, such as, "I can read French but cannot speak or write it well."

Overseas Study, Travel, or Residence

Hiring officials may place considerable weight on responses provided in this category. Evidence of travel experience or overseas study indicates that the applicant is interested in other cultures and is adaptable to living conditions different from those in the United States. Educators with prior overseas experience typically will find the transition to a new location easier to handle. Not only will they be less likely to experience severe culture shock, but they also will be familiar with the mechanics of obtaining passports, visas, customs forms, and foreign currency, which may mean less work for the employer. Applicants should capitalize on any living experience outside the United States, no matter how long ago it may have occurred.

Open-Ended Questions

Many application forms include open-ended questions. It is always to the applicant's advantage to respond to these questions, even though they may be designated as optional. Responses to open-ended questions should be used to elaborate on information listed in another section of the application form or to introduce relevant material that is not covered in any other section. Typical open-ended questions include the following:

Why did you choose a career in education?

What strengths can you bring to our school?

Describe skills and abilities you think you will need to make a contribution in an overseas teaching environment.

Why do you want to teach in this part of the world?

What is your philosophy of education?

Describe yourself as a teacher, or tell how your students would describe you.

Open-ended questions provide an opportunity to indicate short- or long-range goals and to demonstrate the ability to express ideas clearly and in proper grammatical style, using complete sentences and appropriate paragraphing. Clarity, conciseness, and correctness of expression are often evaluated as carefully as the content of the responses.

Final Notes About Application Forms

Walid Abushakra, Superintendent of the Universal American School in Khaldiyah, Kuwait, encourages candidates for overseas jobs to be honest about answering all questions on application forms and to provide all information requested. Because administrators must screen applications so carefully in order to avoid hiring a teacher who will not be an asset to their staff and community, complete and accurate information is a necessity. Many application forms require applicants to certify with their signature that the information contained in the form is accurate, and that any false or misleading information could lead to termination of any contractual agreement between the applicant and the employer. As Mr. Abushakra points out: "The teacher is going to be the victim if the recruiter makes a mistake in evaluation."

It is not unusual for the application form to provide instructions as to other documents the applicant must submit, either with the completed form or under separate cover. Documents typically requested may include copies of certificates; official transcripts of college credits; and copies of the references contained in the applicant's placement file. The applicant should retain a copy of the completed application form for future reference; it may be useful for review before an interview or as an aid in completing applications from other overseas schools.

EVALUATION FORMS

Applicants should be aware that many international schools have devised their own forms to gather personal as well as professional evaluations of potential staff members. After applications have been received and screened, it is not unusual for the employer to request a written evaluation from some of the references listed on the application form. Applicants can expect that persons listed as references will receive a form similar to the sample at right.

EVALUATION FORM

_____(Applicant's name)_____ has applied for a teaching or administrative position and has given your name as a reference. Candidates are selected on the basis of academic and professional qualifications and experience, a personal interview, and the references submitted on their behalf. Your frank statement concerning the candidate's personality traits and professional ability will be appreciated and will be considered strictly confidential. Please return this form promptly via Air Mail.

PROFESSIONAL ABILITY	Superior	Average	Poor	No Knowledge
Academic Preparation				
Classroom Control				
Ability to individualize instruction				
Daily Preparation				
Innovation/Creativity				
Reliability				
Cooperation & Rapport with students & staff				
PERSONALITY TRAITS				
Appearance/Grooming				
Emotional Stability				
Adaptability/Flexibility				
Health/Physical Stamina				
Trustworthiness				
Resourcefulness				
Community Activity				

continued

(continued from previous page)

How long have you known this applicant professionally?

Would you hire this person to teach a child of yours? Why or why not?

Will this applicant contribute beyond required duties? If yes, how has this been demonstrated?

In your judgment, does the applicant's interest in foreign employment represent a desire to escape personal or professional problems (e.g., marital difficulties, emotional disturbance, alcoholism, financial difficulty, etc.)?

Additional remarks:

An applicant might think of the evaluation form as the equivalent of the common stateside practice whereby the prospective employer telephones a previous or current administrator for a candid in-depth appraisal of the applicant's professional abilities and personal behavior. Awkward and embarrassing situations can be avoided if applicants always inform current administrators of their decision to seek overseas employment before submitting their names. Administrators should also be informed that the prospective employer may request that they complete an evaluation form. These forms are usually considered confidential, and applicants should not ask or expect to receive a copy of the evaluation.

HALFWAY THERE

Developing and designing a résumé or vita, writing individual cover letters, obtaining letters of recommendation, and completing application forms constitute perhaps the most time-consuming stage of the overseas job search. Critical decisions are based on these documents; hiring officials use them to select from the pool of applicants those who will be given further consideration. Applicants who thoroughly understand the purpose and use of these documents and who put their best efforts into their preparation will find that this paperwork will bring them one step closer to their ultimate goal.

I assume that all candidates are knowledgeable teachers; therefore, I concentrate on the chemistry of the interview to assist me in choosing people who I feel would fit into our school and community.

Clifford H. Strommen
Lusaka, Zambia

The importance of how you present yourself at interviews through dress and grooming cannot be overstated.

Thomas J. Rushcamp
Jeddah, Saudi Arabia

Generally, in order to set the applicants at ease I ask that they tell me what they have been doing for the last few years. An attempt is made to let the interviewee talk without my asking questions, since this may tell me more about the candidate than any set of questions will determine.

Milt Pavlina
São Paulo, Brazil

Candidates are usually "up" for the interview and excited by the prospect of going overseas. As a result, some hear only what they want to hear and miss or ignore information which should be discussed and clarified.

Richard C. Chesley
Monrovia, Liberia

Chapter Four

Interviewing—Thirty Minutes That Can Change Your Life

The importance of the interview for positions in overseas schools and colleges cannot be overemphasized. Recruiters and applicants both agree that their single most significant contact is the personal interview. No matter how suitable the applicant may appear to be on paper, the interview is the primary determining factor in the selection process. Because recalls or second interviews for overseas teaching positions are rare, the applicant must approach each interview as a first and last chance to demonstrate the ability to assume the responsibilities of the particular position; to function well and harmoniously within the school and community; and to adapt to new situations, unfamiliar surroundings, and unusual circumstances.

RECRUITMENT PRACTICES IN ELEMENTARY AND SECONDARY EDUCATION

Compared to the average American school district, most international schools spend disproportionate amounts of time and money in the recruitment and selection of new staff members. Preinterview contacts, an extended recruiting trip, postinterview follow-ups, and predeparture arrangements and correspondence typically consume inordinate amounts of time. In addition to the expense of recruiting trips to the United States, relocation costs including transportation for the educator (and perhaps for dependents), shipping costs for household goods and other personal possessions, and the "settling-in" of new arrivals may represent an investment of several thousand dollars even before the new staff member is officially on salary. In light of these expenses, it is understandable that administrators of international schools view the selection process very seriously and make every possible effort to hire the best candidate for the position—one who will make a satisfactory adjustment to the new situation and who will fulfill the terms of the contract.

Although large international schools sometimes employ personnel directors or hire stateside representatives to screen prospective teachers and administrators, most often the recruiter is the school's chief administrator, who may have the title of Superintendent, Director, Headmaster or Headmistress, or simply Head. The president or another designated representative of the school's governing body usually will conduct interviews for chief administrative positions. Regardless of the title, recruiters for international schools are seldom rookies; most are well-educated and highly skilled professionals who will use the interview to measure carefully the applicant's strengths and weaknesses.

Interviewing styles differ widely. Some recruiters prefer a structured or directive style in which they clearly control the interview. Others may expect the applicant to take an active role and do much of the talking. Whatever the interviewer's style, the applicant must be prepared to respond appropriately to general and specific questions and, in turn, to formulate and pose intelligent questions as the opportunity arises.

The process of interviewing and selecting teachers and support personnel is often considered one of the most important administrative functions. Nearly all recruiters, however, have multiple responsibilities. In addition to personnel recruiting, administrators are responsible for the operation of their schools and must be actively involved in decisions regarding budget, curriculum, purchasing, supervision and staff development, and relations between the school and the host country. Routine duties may be delegated during the recruiter's stateside trip, but the weight of responsibility follows the administrator around the world.

In a typical recruiting visit to the United States, an administrator will participate in one or more educational conferences, travel thousands of miles, attend to personal and professional business, and interview dozens or even hundreds of qualified applicants at recruiting fairs or placement offices, in hotels and restaurants, and even sometimes in airport terminals. Schedules are hectic and time is limited, but, because many of the administrators will work directly with the people they hire, they are thoroughly committed to selecting educators who will be both productive and congenial colleagues.

RECRUITMENT PRACTICES IN HIGHER EDUCATION

Educators who have sought faculty or staff positions in American colleges and universities are familiar with standard recruiting procedures that typically involve an intensive on-campus interview lasting several hours or even more than one day. It is not unusual for the applicant to talk with a number of individuals, including administrators, faculty members, and students, who together constitute a search committee. Members of the search committee are usually responsible for evaluating the interview performance of finalists and recommending the chosen candidate to the hiring official. As a part of the scheduled interview, finalists are often expected to present a lecture or to conduct a class. On-campus visits also give the applicant the opportunity to meet with potential colleagues and students, to inspect research facilities, and to tour the campus and the community.

Recruitment practices for overseas college and university positions often differ markedly from the practices followed by stateside institutions of higher education. Applicants for positions in foreign countries are more likely to meet with only one individual for a relatively brief period of time. The setting for the interview may be an American campus, but it may also be a hotel room in a metropolitan area or the office of the foreign college's stateside representative.

Because for most foreign colleges it is financially infeasible to send heads of individual departments to the United States for extended recruiting visits, colleges often employ a stateside representative to conduct their interviews. The representative may be employed by a single university or may serve as a consultant for several foreign institutions. Such an individual may hold a faculty position in an American college or university or may be a nonacademic who has strong ties to the university or business interests in the country. When stateside representatives are used, the employing institution typically relies on the vita, supporting documents, and references to evaluate the candidate's professional competencies and pedagogical skills. The interviewer's task is principally aimed at evaluating the applicant's personality, stability, and adaptability.

Foreign colleges and universities sometimes dispense with the face-to-face interview. Instead, an interview may be conducted by telephone, or the employing institution may rely solely on contacts between the job applicant and a long-distance network of professional connections. To illustrate how a network might operate, let us assume that a vacancy exists at Xenophilos University. Wherever this university might be, there is a good chance that at least one of its faculty members has received one or more graduate degrees from a United States university. This faculty member makes use of the network by contacting a stateside mentor, adviser, or colleague who then confers with the applicant and relays information back to the overseas employer for evaluation.

Colleges and universities with a large number of job openings may send a college administrator or faculty member, or even a recruiting team, to conduct stateside interviews. Interviews conducted by a team of recruiters are usually lengthier and more comprehensive than those conducted by a third party and more closely resemble their stateside equivalent. Certainly, the recruiting team will be able to provide the applicant with more detailed, firsthand information about the specific vacancy, the institution, and the community.

Whether the applicant is selected on the basis of a network, a telephone interview, or an interview conducted by a recruiting team or other representative, an important difference between the selection practices of foreign universities and the practices of most American colleges and universities is the lack of intensive advance interaction between the candidate selected and the colleagues and administrators with whom the new faculty member will work.

WHAT DO INTERVIEWERS LOOK FOR?

Recruiters will use the personal interview to confirm or negate impressions conveyed by the applicant's résumé and other written communications. In the process, they will also attempt to assess the applicant's personality and to make a decision about the applicant's suitability for the overseas position. Most international recruiters, like good recruiters anywhere, generally try to alleviate interview anxiety as quickly as possible and to make the applicant feel comfortable and at ease. Skilled interviewers can deftly lead applicants through a conversation that may appear to be a spontaneous discussion of topics of mutual interest and concern. In spite of the casual atmosphere the interviewer may be able to create, most recruiters have carefully prepared a list of questions from which they select appropriate items. They do this in an effort to make the most effective use of the limited time allotted to each applicant. A list of possible interview questions generally will include some inquiries that are designed to elicit specific, factual information and some that could lead to an in-depth discussion of subject matter, pedagogy, or personal philosophies.

QUESTIONS INTERVIEWERS MAY ASK

What qualifications do you have that make you a good candidate for teaching in another country?

Tell me about your present position.

What kinds of problems have you encountered in your current assignment?

What curriculum programs have you used?

Describe how you individualize your lessons or assignments.

What supplementary materials do you find most helpful?

How do you use the school's learning resource center?

If I visited your class, what could I expect to find?

Are you willing to team teach?

Could you handle three or more preparations at the secondary level?

Have you ever worked with students for whom English is a second or third language?

Interviewing

As an elementary teacher, can you handle instruction in physical education, art, and music?

As an art teacher, could you be happy teaching both elementary and secondary students?

How do you view the role of the principal?

What kind of person was your last principal to work with?

What, if anything, would you change about your current principal?

How do you think you would work with people whose ethical standards are different from your own?

How do you feel about grades as a measure of student achievement?

Would it ever be possible for all students in your class to receive the same grade?

Why are you thinking about leaving your present position?

What types of activities did you participate in when you were in high school? in college?

How did you choose your major?

In what professional assignments would you be especially interested?

What extracurricular activities can you sponsor or coach?

What previous experience have you had with extracurricular activities?

Give examples of motivation techniques you find most effective.

How do you communicate with parents about a student's progress?

How do you use support personnel such as counselors, librarians, psychologists, etc.?

What kind of disciplinary techniques do you use?

Have you ever referred a student to the principal for disciplinary reasons?

When did you decide to pursue an overseas career?

How do your spouse, parents, and children feel about your decision?

What books have you read in the last six months?

What is your favorite TV program?

Tell me about previous travel experiences.

Do you have any physical problems requiring regular medical attention?

What do you expect to gain from an experience in international living?

What do you expect to have to give up?

Is your spouse a teacher?

Tell me about teachers you have had who have had the most influence on you.

What do you find most and least satisfactory about teaching as a career?

Do you prefer to work with students of low, average, or superior academic ability? If you have a preference, why?

Name five qualities of a good teacher.

When did you decide to become a teacher?

What do you expect to be doing five years from now?

Questions such as these are obviously not designed to elicit responses that can be identified as "correct" or "incorrect." Rather, by allowing the applicant considerable latitude in formulating a response, the recruiter hopes to be able to identify aspects of experience, character, judgment, and motivation similar to those exhibited by successful educators in international schools. To help applicants understand what employers are looking for, ten sample questions are presented below, followed by notes illustrating the recruiter's purpose in asking the questions and the types of responses being sought.

Why do you want to go overseas? Nearly every recruiter asks this question at some point in the interview. Although short, direct, and apparently easy to answer, it is a multifaceted question whose answer will give the recruiter a number of insights into the applicant's motivations and initiative. Interviewers are interested in individuals who have a desire to travel and to experience other cultures, to work with a variety of people, to extend their subject expertise through educational growth and development, and to meet new challenges. Any or all of these reasons would constitute a favorable response, since all of them are valid reasons that have been expressed by people who have successfully worked abroad. Ambiguous responses may serve as a warning signal to the recruiter that the applicant has not given adequate thought to the decision to pursue a career abroad, is trying to escape a personal problem, or has been unable to secure satisfactory employment at home. Interviewers are not looking for a rehearsed answer, but any applicant who is unable to provide a thoughtful, articulate response to this basic question will not be considered a good prospect for success in an overseas school.

Why do you want to come to our country? Responses to this question can reveal the extent of the applicant's knowledge of or research into various facets of the specific country, including such aspects as its location and climate, customs and life-style, and language and culture. Employers do not necessarily expect an applicant to know a great deal about their school and community. Nevertheless, they will always be favorably impressed if the applicant has taken the time to learn as much as possible about the host country, the community, and the school. The recruiter will, of course, want to know if the applicant has had any firsthand acquaintance with the country as a result of previous travel or study, or if the applicant has had contact with other people who have lived or traveled extensively in the area. Interviewers have the right to expect that applicants will at least know where the country is located; lack of such basic knowledge usually will eliminate the applicant from serious consideration.

Tell me about yourself. The purpose of such a simple, open-ended inquiry is to elicit responses that will enable the interviewer to form a sense of how applicants view themselves and their experiences and how they see the relevance of these experiences in the context of an overseas job. Recruiters usually have had the opportunity to review the applicant's résumé or vita and other papers, and this type of question is not intended to elicit a rehash or simple summary of the applicant's educational background or professional experience. The interviewer is instead looking for the kind of information that does not ordinarily appear in professional documents and can only be obtained in a direct, personal encounter. Interviewers know that the most desirable candidates are those who possess qualities of flexibility, adaptability, self-reliance, self-confidence, and open-mindedness. In addition, responses that demonstrate the candidate's ability to work, travel, or live independently are viewed positively. Citing specific examples of previous activities or associations with different ethnic or cultural groups either in the United States or abroad can be very helpful in this context. It is important to remember, however, that while recruiters are definitely interested in knowing if the applicant has had any exposure to foreign cultures either at home or abroad, they also want to know about other kinds of experiences. Applicants sometimes make the mistake of attempting to concentrate only on activities or experiences that seem to relate directly to working abroad; in doing so, they overlook the significance and essential relevance of such basic experiences as attending a college or university far from home or accepting a teaching position in a setting different from the one they are accustomed to. Moving from a small town to an urban setting, from a metropolitan area to a rural community, or to any location that removes a person from a familiar environment and the immediate support of family and longtime acquaintances can illustrate desirable qualities of independence and adaptability.

Do you have any idea about the living conditions in our part of the world? Recruiters who pose a direct question about the living conditions in a specific international community generally have a dual purpose in mind: to discover the applicant's expectations and priorities and to determine the extent of the applicant's basic knowledge of conditions in order to help revise or augment that knowledge. Interviewers appreciate that the spirit of romance and adventure often may motivate applicants to consider foreign teaching opportunities; but they are also well aware that only applicants who are realistically informed about the day-to-day living conditions are likely to make a comfortable and satisfactory adjustment. In underdeveloped parts of the world, food supplies, clothing, and other necessities frequently are difficult to obtain on the open market. In areas of widespread poverty, the poor are not neatly tucked away in ghettos but are highly visible. In some countries thievery may be a potential problem for an outsider who is not wary and alert. An interviewer knows that a naive foreigner who is poorly informed about the local culture, mores, and standard of living may find the adjustment to this kind of living situation difficult and initially traumatic. Conversely, in highly developed countries, economic conditions may not allow for a standard of living compatible with the applicant's expectations. Typically, food, housing, fuel, appliances, and utilities and other services will account for a significantly larger portion of an educator's earnings than they do in the United States. This may leave less money for travel and other leisure activities than applicants anticipate.

Recruiters are aware that not all candidates are able to obtain detailed information about specifics of daily living, but they do expect that the candidate will have obtained basic information about economic and social conditions. At the same time, interviewers want the applicant to be honest and straightforward; they do not want applicants to try to appear more knowledgeable and informed than they really are. Recruiters would far rather be asked for specific information than to have applicants minimize the importance of the question or attempt to bluff their way through a response.

How do you spend time away from school? Because relocating overseas removes educators from familiar settings, friends, family members, and support systems, recruiters often want to know how applicants spend their leisure time. Applicants with no identifiable leisure interests may have a difficult time finding evening or weekend activities to occupy them once they are settled in their overseas environment. Interviewers are, of course, always interested in learning of outside interests that correspond with extracurricular activities sponsored by the school. In general, however, the exact nature of a leisure activity is usually less important than the mere fact that the applicant has developed some hobby or outside interest that can be pursued in the host country. Recruiters know that idleness can easily lead to boredom, loneliness, and dissatisfaction, and that applicants with transferable leisure skills or interests, such as stamp collecting, gourmet cooking, photography, or individual sports, may be able to adjust more easily to a new setting. On the other hand, avid film buffs or television addicts may encounter difficulties in parts of the world where movie theaters or television programming are limited.

How would your students describe you? This question is used by interviewers to explore both the applicant's image of the educator's role and ability to empathize with students. In particular, the interviewer will be looking for information that reveals the types of relationships the educator has formed with students inside and outside the classroom; student reactions to classroom activities; and specific interpersonal skills, together with characteristics such as fairness, consistency, and a sense of humor. Although applicants have a good deal of latitude in responding to a question of this type, recruiters are impressed by people who show that they have taken the time to consider how they are viewed by their students and who can realistically assess the judgments that students might make.

What are your strengths and weaknesses as an educator? The most successful teachers are those who are able to identify those things they do well and diagnose areas that could be improved. Interviewers use questions about strengths and weaknesses to assess an applicant's self-perception and to confirm written evaluations or comments from references or former employers. It is essential for faculty members in overseas schools to work cooperatively with each other and with the administration, and recruiters will be especially interested in applicants who represent themselves as good team members. Because the international school is often the focal point of the American community, diplomacy and the ability to build and maintain good interpersonal relationships with parents and other community members are especially important. Interviewers are also looking for indications that teachers enjoy their students as well as their subject matter and consider themselves effective role models. Candidates who can articulate experiences and attitudes that demonstrate qualities of patience, sensitivity, and acceptance of individual differences are preferred.

While it is easier and more pleasant to identify strengths, employers are equally interested in perceived weaknesses. Interviewers understand that applicants will tend to be very guarded about revealing shortcomings in their personality or teaching styles, but they appreciate the applicant who has thought about methods of improving competencies, skills, and relationships and has taken some steps to strengthen or correct deficiencies or problem areas. Examples of the kind of shortcomings that might be cited include taking on too many responsibilities at one time, allowing students too much latitude in meeting deadlines or requirements, or not organizing time efficiently enough to allow for the regular reading of professional literature. Interviewers are looking for educators whose responses to this question reveal the ability to identify and solve problems and to concentrate on positive rather than negative approaches.

What kind of learning environment do you try to create? This question is meant to elicit information in a number of different areas, ranging from the concrete to the abstract and philosophical. Responses may include discussions of such tangible items as seating arrangements, decoration of the classroom, and use of bulletin boards or other visual display devices. Interviewers typically are also interested in the type of atmosphere the teacher tries to create, whether quiet and orderly or bustling with controlled enthusiasm. Applicants reveal much about their teaching philosophy and techniques by the way they describe their classroom setting and activities.

What types of teaching aids or visuals do you need in order to conduct your classes? Answers to questions about teaching aids and supplies not only define what the applicant feels is necessary to be a productive staff member but also allow the teacher to give examples of innovation and creativity. Interviewers may also ask this question in order to determine how the applicant's estimated need for teaching materials compares with what the school currently has available or has the means to obtain. Long-range planning is frequently necessary in this area, because even if resources for new materials are readily available, the combined factors of distance and import regulations often may result in considerable delays before the new materials reach the school. In addition, interviewers may be particularly impressed by teachers who exhibit the imagination and creative skills needed to produce some of their own teaching aids or supplementary visual materials.

The unspoken question: Will you be a good representative of the United States? This is a question that in all likelihood will never be asked aloud but is of primary concern to recruiters at every stage of the selection process. As such, it will be the single most important question to be answered indirectly through the interview. From their own experience, recruiters know that—like it or not—educators working overseas are ambassadors of their home country. In spite of what we know about individual differences and pluralistic societies, we all tend to be influenced by the people whom we actually encounter, whether we meet them socially or merely see them pass by. Americans traveling abroad, and especially those who may be living and working in one location for an extended period, must accept the responsibility of serving as representatives of American society, culture, and morality. International schools are best served by staff members who can willingly and graciously assume this burden. Superpatriotism and flag-waving are neither required nor even desirable responses, but educators are expected to be knowledgeable about and capable of an intelligent discussion of American values and ideals; insincerity and naiveté are perhaps the least pardonable shortcomings. Administrators of international schools are keenly sensitive about the impression their staff members create within the host country. No recruiter wants to be responsible for introducing, perpetuating, or reviving the image of the "Ugly American." Recruiters simply cannot afford to risk being embarrassed or let down by staff members who are unable or unwilling to be positive representatives of their own country while adapting to the culture and routine of the local community.

AN INTERVIEW IS MORE THAN A SERIES OF RESPONSES

Many applicants share a common misconception that the interview is a test, consisting of a series of questions to which the applicant must respond. Certainly the recruiter's questions are important, but the applicant must never lose sight of the fact that an interview should be a mutual exchange. The applicant should not play a merely passive role responding to stimuli from the interviewer; rather, the applicant must play a very active role presenting a professional image from the first moment of the interview through its conclusion. A professional image is multidimensional; it is reflected not only in what applicants say but in the nature of their appearance, conduct, and manner of speaking.

Positive first impressions are critical to successful interviewing. It is undoubtedly an exaggeration to claim, as some people do, that the decision to hire is made during the first two minutes of the interview. More likely, the decision not to hire is made in the first several minutes. Negative first impressions can rarely be overcome, but positive first impressions can be diminished as the interview progresses. More people talk themselves out of jobs than into them.

Appearance

The professional image conveyed by the applicant begins with personal grooming and attire. Before the recruiter has an opportunity to ask even the most basic question, impressions are created by the applicant's physical appearance. Fortunately, this aspect of the professional image is one of the easiest to control, although it may require careful thought and some expense. Recruiters generally tend to dress well, and they expect a businesslike, professional appearance of their potential staff members. Because interview days can be long, applicants should select clothing that will remain comfortable and neat-looking even after several hours. A suit and tie for men and a suit or dress for women are correct and desirable attire. Selecting unusual fashions or bizarre designs may create a negative impression and may make the applicant feel and look out of place. The safest and best approach is the one recommended by Robert Iannuzzelli, Superintendent of the American School in Hawalli, Kuwait: "At interviews, dress relatively conservatively—and smile!"

Conduct

It is a cliché to say "be yourself" at interviews, but the advice is sound. Candidates need not work at trying to impress the interviewer; it will happen naturally if the candidate is adequately prepared, remains relaxed, and feels quietly confident about interviewing skills and etiquette. Most recruiters have conducted enough interviews to have developed the sixth sense that enables them to spot a phony. Few people can successfully portray attitudes and behaviors that have not developed naturally as the result of their background and experiences—especially in the unfamiliar or tense atmosphere that may exist in an interview situation.

Personality traits are revealed in many ways, both in words and actions. Interview behavior should demonstrate that the applicant is assertive but not aggressive, self-confident but not arrogant, personable but not chummy, motivated but not overzealous. Although interview behavior is an individual matter, interview etiquette is universal. Appropriate behavior may take a variety of forms, but inappropriate actions are clearly and easily defined:

DO NOT choose a "native costume" or faddish clothing

DO NOT arrive "fashionably" late

DO NOT bring family members (unless otherwise instructed)

DO NOT initiate a handshake

DO NOT sit until invited

DO NOT fidget

DO NOT use the recruiter's first name (especially without invitation)

DO NOT smoke or chew gum

DO NOT boast or brag

DO NOT fill quiet spaces with idle talk

DO NOT try to be funny

DO NOT answer in monosyllables

DO NOT monopolize the conversation

DO NOT argue

DO NOT shout or whisper

DO NOT speak negatively of previous employers

DO NOT introduce the topic of salary

DO NOT take notes

DO NOT keep checking your watch

As obvious as this list of prohibitions may appear, recruiters regularly encounter each and every action mentioned. A certain amount of nervousness and anxiety is to be expected considering the importance of the interview; this brief encounter may indeed change the course of an applicant's professional career and personal life. Applicants can reduce the chances of inadvertently displaying inappropriate, anxiety-induced behaviors by planning ahead, by concentrating on the recruiter, and by listening carefully during the course of the interview.

Manner of Speaking

Applicants can reinforce their professional image not only by what they say but by how they say it. Applicants should familiarize themselves with the basics of effective oral communication—audibility, articulation, and tone. Nervous mannerisms in the form of uneven speech patterns, breathy tones, and fillers such as "er," "uh," or "you know" diminish the value of spoken responses. Some of these patterns can be overcome by working with a tape recorder to become aware of any distracting habits or mannerisms in one's speech patterns. Practicing interviews with a friend or colleague also may be helpful and gives the applicant the chance to receive immediate, constructive feedback.

In addition to the mechanics of speech production, applicants need to pay attention to vocabulary and phrasing. Just as the résumé depends on active words to convey a sense of achievement, the applicant must rely on well-chosen words in oral communication to convey a sense of enthusiasm and professional competency. Here, too, using active words such as *created, designed, accomplished, initiated,* and *motivated* will serve to represent the applicant as a dynamic and committed professional. Finally, applicants need to develop the habit of phrasing responses positively. This is especially important when discussing current or previous work experiences or employers, administrators, colleagues, and students. Speaking negatively of an experience raises questions in the listener's mind about the applicant's ability to cooperate, to adjust to situations, or to be a flexible team member.

PREPARING AN INTERVIEW SURVIVAL KIT

Preparing an Interview Survival Kit containing professional and personal materials may help to facilitate the interview process while serving to enhance an applicant's professional image. An Interview Survival Kit can be a useful accessory whether the applicant is meeting with a single interviewer in a placement office or hotel or is attending an organized recruiting fair, with interviews scheduled over a period of several hours or even several days. Regardless of the interview arrangements, applicants must be prepared for unexpected delays, last-minute cancellations, and some inconvenience. Long waits and crowded facilities need not affect the applicant's interview performance if such inconveniences have been anticipated and provisions have been made.

The Survival Kit should be easy to carry and unobtrusive; attaché cases, bookbags, or flight bags are serviceable and appropriate for this purpose. The kit should be organized into two sections. The professional section is intended to demonstrate to the interviewer that the applicant is organized and efficient by providing documentation, verification, or illustration of topics discussed during the interview. Because interview time is limited, it is not advisable to assemble an extensive portfolio containing detailed lesson plans or videotapes. Rather, any materials presented should be easy for the interviewer to absorb quickly, and the applicant should plan to use them only when they contribute directly to the discussion at hand. Before presenting these materials it is essential to judge the appropriateness of the item, to consider the interest level of the interviewer, and to weigh the benefits to be gained by their use against the amount of time it will take. Obviously, the materials must be organized so that they are easily accessible during the course of the interview.

Personal materials are included in the Survival Kit to help applicants stay alert and refreshed throughout the entire day. At a recruiting fair, applicants may have a gap of several hours between interview appointments. Snacks can sustain energy if food services are not readily available, and a book or other reading material can help minimize the frustrations and anxieties that may accumulate during a lengthy wait. Grooming aids can help an applicant to make as satisfactory a first impression at the last interview of the day as at the first.

ASKING INTELLIGENT QUESTIONS

Because the interview is an exchange of information and impressions, applicants must prepare to respond to questions from the recruiter and must also be prepared to pose intelligent questions of their own. As an experienced recruiter, Thomas Rushcamp offers this advice to prospective overseas educators: "Your questions tell me a great deal about yourself—choose them with care and do not ask too many."

During the initial stages of the job search, most applicants have uncovered basic information about the host country, the community, and perhaps even the specific school to which they have applied, through research at libraries or by talking with individuals who have firsthand information. This knowledge bank should provide the applicant with a solid basis from which to develop a list of specific questions. Recruiters expect that an applicant will have formulated general questions about the social customs and living conditions in the country as well as professional questions concerning the school and its curriculum and philosophies, and therefore they routinely offer this information in the earliest stages of the interview. Applicants need to be aware that interview time is limited and will allow for only a few questions. To make the best use of interview time applicants are encouraged to prioritize questions so that critical inquiries can be made at the appropriate time. It is to the applicant's advantage to let the conversation flow without frequent interruption. When the opportunity arises, questions may be asked either to acquire information or to confirm facts or impressions. Applicants need to understand that the recruiter will use the applicant's questions as another means of evaluation—applicants who have no questions or those who have far too many may weaken their position.

Listed below is a sampling of typical questions that educators seeking overseas jobs might ask during the interview. For applicants who have secured considerable information about the host country, many of these questions may be useful merely as a preinterview review. For applicants who have been unable to obtain current literature or to make contact with individuals who are well acquainted with the country, such questions may help identify areas where essential information will be needed.

Questions for All Applicants

If housing is not provided, what options are available?

How does the cost of living in the host country compare to the United States?

How are Americans received by the local population?

Is the government politically stable?

How large is the American community?

What types of cultural and/or recreational activities are available?

What medical facilities are available within the community?

Are there special health precautions or potential problems that I should be aware of?

What about accessibility of transportation?

Are there organized trips to other countries (students/staff)?

Why is the position open?

What is the typical yearly turnover of staff?

How do your facilities compare to a typical suburban school in the United States?

Are budgets allocated for each department?

When do you anticipate making a decision?

How will I be notified?

Questions About Salaries and Benefits

Questions related to salary and benefits are an important part of the interview exchange. Although the candidate should not initiate this discussion, once the recruiter has introduced the topic it is entirely appropriate for the applicant to ask questions to ensure a thorough understanding of the financial arrangements. Salaries and benefits are usually covered late in the interview, and time may not permit a lengthy explanation of all aspects of the compensation package. The time to obtain detailed information is after the contract is offered.

What is the salary (or salary range) for this position?

Are salaries paid in U.S. dollars or in the currency of the host country?

Does the contract contain an inflation clause tied to U.S. or host-country inflation rates?

In addition to salary, what benefits are offered (retirement, medical/dental plans, leaves, etc.)?

Are salaries subject to U.S. and/or local taxes?

What is the length of the commitment (one year, three years, etc.)?

Are transportation costs and shipping expenses included in the contract?

Does the contract provide for transportation for dependents? home leaves? other travel?

Does the contract contain an evacuation clause?

Is there a relocation or settling-in allowance?

Are staff members extended PX privileges, embassy club privileges, etc.?

Questions for Elementary or Secondary School Teachers

Applicants for elementary or secondary teaching positions should formulate a number of general and specific questions concerning the assignment, the curriculum, and the school. Questions might include any of the following:

What is the typical class size?

What types of students are enrolled?

Do students often enter or leave during the academic year?

What is the ratio of students to teachers?

What is the ratio of American children to those of other nationalities attending the school?

Are there special language classes for students who are not native English speakers?

Are instructional materials (library books, construction paper, films, etc.) easily accessible?

Are there specific instructional materials I should plan to bring with me?

In addition to teachers, what special support personnel are employed by the school?

Are faculty members expected to participate in or sponsor extracurricular activities?

What types of extracurricular activities are offered?

How many students go on to college, and where do they go?

Are parents active in school activities and functions?

Questions for College and University Professors

The types of questions applicants for college and university positions should ask may be largely determined by who is conducting the interview. Recruiters who are stateside representatives may possess only limited specific information about curriculum or the responsibilities of the position. If the interviewer actually comes from the overseas institution, many of the following questions may be appropriate:

What level of students will I work with (undergraduate, graduate)?

How are students evaluated (examinations, papers)?

Will I report to the department head? to the dean?

Who is responsible for evaluating my work?

Will I be expected to maintain office hours in addition to teaching?

Are there opportunities for committee involvement?

If English is the language of instruction, what problems should I expect to encounter with non-native speakers?

What research facilities are available for faculty use?

How many faculty members hold doctoral degrees?

Where did most faculty members obtain their degrees?

How many students typically pursue graduate degrees and where do they go?

What library facilities are available?

What class size can I expect?

How many students are enrolled in this department?

Are there any policies or restrictions regarding personal or professional activities of which I should be aware?

Questions for Administrators

Educators seeking overseas administrative posts will need to receive detailed information on a number of topics, ranging from day-to-day school operations to relationships with school board representatives, staff members, and community members. Reading fact sheets and other information provided by the school board will help the job applicant obtain a great deal of this information, some of which may need further clarification and amplification during the interview. Any of the following questions might be relevant:

What is the governing body of the school and how is it selected?

How is the school financed (tuition, corporate funding, private donations)?

Who is responsible for formulating and administering the budget?

What is the current administrative staff?

How long have these people been in their positions?

How many certificated and noncertificated people are currently employed?

What is the turnover rate for professional staff?

Have there been or do you expect significant changes in the number of students enrolled?

What are current standards or requirements for admission (tuition, English-speaking ability, test scores, nationality, etc.)?

Has discipline been a problem?

Are local municipal or government officials cooperative and supportive of the school?

Have there been any problems in obtaining needed supplies?

Have past administrators taken an active role in orienting new staff members to the community?

Are staff members responsible for finding their own housing or does the school provide assistance?

Are there any staff problems that I should be aware of?

What types of extracurricular programs are offered? How many students participate in them?

Are facilities adequate for the various instructional and extracurricular programs?

Is the school the focal point of the American community?

Does the school have an open-door policy for community activities?

Questions for Educators with Dependents

Educators who will be accompanied by dependents have special considerations that need to be explored during the interview. Applicants might consider asking any of these questions:

Are there employment opportunities for my spouse?

Do any current faculty or staff members have nonteaching spouses?

What activities or clubs are available for nonteaching, nonworking spouses?

From past experience, have most nonworking spouses enjoyed living in your city?

Does the school provide day-care facilities for dependent children?

Have most grade school children of staff members adjusted to the community and school in the past?

Are there special items I should plan to take along for my children (medicines, prescriptions, clothing, toys, etc.)?

Is tuition provided for staff members' children?

Will I be treated differently in the community as a single parent?

Are dependents covered under your health plan?

Is the salary adequate for a family of four to live on?

Is housing easily obtainable for a couple with children?

CONCLUDING REMARKS

Before leaving the interview, candidates need to find out exactly what is expected of them, especially with regard to any additional documents that must be submitted or application procedures that must be followed. Applicants also should ask what they can expect of the interviewer with regard to being informed of a hiring decision. In turn, the recruiter should be assured of the applicant's desire to be considered for the available position. A brief expression of appreciation and continued interest will leave recruiters with the impression that they have just interviewed an enthusiastic and socially adept professional.

AFTER THE INTERVIEW

The time immediately following the interview can be just as important as the time spent in preparation for it. The postinterview period should be used wisely;

applicants should not waste the first few minutes trying to predict the outcome of the interview or critiquing every minute detail of their interview performance. If possible, they should find a quiet place and take notes about the various subjects discussed during the preceding thirty or forty minutes.

Taking the time to make some objective notes about the conversation will help applicants avoid the common pitfall of remembering only what they want to remember and ignoring less positive aspects of the encounter. In addition to making notes about specific details and any directives or requests for further action, applicants should jot down any topics that were introduced but not thoroughly discussed and any items omitted that should have been covered. At a recruiting fair it is especially important that these notes be recorded immediately after the interview to avoid memory lapses or confusion about which recruiter discussed what, when, and where. These notes will be invaluable references for further discussion of specific details if a contract is offered.

After taking notes about the information shared, applicants can then turn their attention to reflecting on their interview performance by asking themselves:

Was I too passive?

Was I too aggressive?

Did I try to entertain rather than inform the recruiter?

Did I monopolize the conversation?

Did I listen carefully?

Did I portray someone I am not?

These questions can serve as the basis for a productive analysis of interview performance and contribute to the formulation of an answer to the most important question: How can I improve my professional image in the next interview?

FOLLOW-UP

No interview is complete until a follow-up letter has been written. Some applicants have the mistaken idea that they should not bother the recruiter with additional paperwork, but the interview follow-up letter is an essential part of the application process, whether it is used to further one's application or to remove one's name from consideration. A follow-up letter not only demonstrates a knowledge of employment etiquette but may be a deciding factor in the selection of the final candidate.

Follow-up letters should be sent within a reasonable time after the interview. The exact timing of a follow-up letter may depend upon how much the applicant knows of the recruiter's stateside itinerary. Recruiters on extended visits to the United States often provide the candidates they interview with their temporary stateside address; when available, this address should be used for the follow-up letter, as has been done in the following example.

SAMPLE INTERVIEW FOLLOW-UP LETTER

```
121 Park Drive
South Bend, Indiana 46628
March 3, 1983
```

```
Dr. George Williamson
American Academy of Cyprus
P.O. Box 6735
Larnaca, Cyprus
```

Dear Dr. Williamson:

I wish to express my continued interest in the principalship
of your elementary school which we discussed in detail at the
Chicago Royal Sheraton Hotel on February 28. As the result
of our conversation regarding the programs and curriculum,
student body, and administrative responsibilities, I am even
more enthusiastic about the prospect of joining your staff.

My experience as an elementary teacher at Caldecott Elementary
School, together with my recent administrative experience, has
provided me with the background to work effectively with
teachers in an open-space, non-graded setting. As you will
recall from our conversation, I have a special interest in
individualized instruction. During the first year of my
present assignment I instituted inservice programs leading to
the implementation of individual education plans (IEP) for
use by each classroom teacher in my building. The program
has been successful, and I would welcome the opportunity to
work with your staff members in developing a similar program.

I appreciate your frank discussion of the unique and challenging
aspects of this position. My previous travel experiences and
my professional background will, I am confident, enable me to
make a strong contribution to the American Academy of Cyprus.

Sincerely,

Melanie Holen

The follow-up letter from Melanie Holen expresses continued interest in the position, shows appreciation for the interviewer's time, and reinforces the applicant's qualifications. Because of the numerous interviews conducted during a stateside recruiting trip, it is important that Melanie has reminded the employer of the exact location and date of the interview.

Follow-up letters are typically brief and to the point. The items mentioned in the initial and concluding paragraphs of Melanie's letter are essential; in most follow-up letters, information comparable to her first and third paragraphs would be sufficient. The middle paragraph of this letter, however, recalls part of the interview conversation and concentrates on Melanie's special interests as they relate specifically to items discussed at the interview.

The tone of the letter is businesslike, even though the actual interview may have been conversational and very informal. The letter illustrates a full block style with all lines beginning exactly at the left margin.

In addition to the information conveyed in this particular sample letter, a follow-up letter may indicate that supporting documents such as college transcripts, additional recommendations, or writing samples are being forwarded to the employer. These materials may be enclosed with the follow-up letter but more often will be sent under separate cover.

Don't panic and jump at the first job offer—investigate the pros and cons.

Gail Zimmerman
Hawalli, Kuwait

Ask questions of friends in appropriate places who have inside information and contacts. Be crystal clear in inquiring about fringes, housing provisions, etc. Know why the job is being offered and what the opinion of your predecessor was.

Gary L. Theisen
Yogyakarta, Indonesia

Don't hesitate to ask questions; don't make a hasty decision. Have a clear understanding of all benefits and services that accompany the job. Have a complete understanding of the monetary system and the products and services your salary will buy in that foreign country.

Michael D. Collins
Dhahran, Saudi Arabia

Do your homework. There are more differences among overseas "American" schools than there are similarities. Be true to yourself and determine the parameters within which you can function effectively.

Curtis C. Harvey
Cali, Colombia

Chapter Five

Decisions and Contracts

Once the interviews are completed, both the recruiter and the applicant enter into another stage of the selection process. Each party must examine many variables in order to arrive at a satisfactory decision; this interim period is a time for serious consideration and careful deliberation. The process of decision-making is not always an easy, clearcut choice between positives and negatives, and the interval between the interview and the offer of a contract can range from just a few days to several months. Experienced educators at all levels characterize this period as a time of emotional highs and lows that can interfere with rational thinking. This chapter explains and illustrates how decisions can be reached and how contracts are offered and acknowledged.

THE EMPLOYER'S MATCHING GAME

The time required for an overseas employer to offer a contract will vary depending upon the number and complexity of decisions that must be made. First, staff needs in specific areas must be considered and finalized. Because many recruiters are not aware of exact needs at the time of their stateside recruiting visit, they often must interview applicants in anticipation of vacancies in particular grade levels and areas of specialization. Contracts cannot be officially offered until current staff members have notified the administrator of their decision not to return. Contracts for returning primary and secondary school teachers typically are offered in March, and the teachers are given a reasonable amount of time (usually about three weeks) to sign and return their contracts, just as in stateside school districts. Once it is determined that a current staff member is leaving, administrators must first consider possible realignments of the existing staff; voluntary transfers or reassignments to a different class or grade level thus can affect the exact hiring needs. Other factors that must be considered by administrators include projected enrollment in the subject area or grade level and sabbatical or maternity leaves requested by current staff members.

Only after such "in-school" decisions have been reached will employers begin the process of assessing and comparing new applicants to find the best possible match for the position. This process may involve checking or rechecking references; it will certainly involve final determinations about each candidate's ability to fit in with the existing staff, to adjust to the school and community, to carry out the responsibilities of the position, and to fulfill the terms of the contract. Once the choice has been narrowed down to one or two top contenders, a contract for the available position will be offered to the preferred candidate via long-distance telephone or even by mail. The chosen candidate will be given adequate time to respond to the offer of the contract. Should the candidate decline the offer, either to accept another offer or to remain in the current teaching position, an offer will then be extended to the second choice. It is possible that a great deal of time may elapse before the final match between the selected candidate and the employing institution becomes a reality.

Contracts are, of course, offered much more quickly in some instances. It is sometimes possible for a recruiter to offer a contract at the conclusion of the interview if the school is expanding rapidly or particular vacancies are known to exist. On-the-spot job offers tend to occur most often among recruiters from schools with large staffs. Such schools sometimes deliberately hire more candidates than they need because they know from experience that a few of those hired will back out of their commitment between the signing of the contract and the time to depart for the overseas assignment. In general, however, most recruiters prefer not to offer contracts on the spot. Waiting until they have finished the interviewing schedule allows them to reflect on all candidates interviewed. Applicants who receive job offers are also better equipped to make a sound decision if they have taken sufficient time to reflect on the available position and their own priorities and preferences. Hasty decisions are more likely to result in broken contracts or dissatisfaction and discontent in the assignment.

THE APPLICANT'S MATCHING GAME

Applicants often feel that once the interview process is completed they are merely engaged in a waiting game, during which employers make all the decisions. Rather than passively waiting to receive a contract offer, however, applicants can use this time profitably to do some matching of their own. Considerable effort should be devoted to reexamining reasons or motivations for going abroad, to reevaluating priorities and preferences, and to reviewing data that has been collected. This additional homework will make it easier to arrive at a sound decision should the applicant receive one or more contract offers.

Contracts may be offered in a number of ways. The offer may be extended over the telephone or in person, be sent by cable or telegram, or be mailed as a registered letter with the contract enclosed. Once an offer has been received, specific questions that were not raised or fully discussed during the interview should now be introduced. At this point in the selection process, the applicant must not be tentative or timid—clarity and straightforwardness by the prospective staff member will serve both parties best in the long run. As David Samore, a teacher formerly employed in Barranquilla, Colombia, suggests, "If you have any questions, ask boldly and bluntly or you are the one who will be deceived; the administrator may not volunteer information about distasteful aspects."

One way to avoid misunderstandings is to prepare in advance to ask all key questions that were not raised during the interview, so that any uncertainties will be fully clarified before the contract is accepted. Experienced international educators also recommend that before signing the contract, applicants ask the administrator of the school for the name and address of a teacher currently employed at the school or one who has recently returned to the United States. Applicants should not be deterred by the expense of long-distance or international telephone calls in such matters. To save time and to allow direct interaction, the telephone is the most efficient and personalized means of contact. Many countries can be dialed direct at reduced costs, and rates during off-hours are often considerably lower. In any case, the amount of money spent is insignificant compared to the total expense of an overseas job search and is far outweighed by the benefits to be gained from talking directly with someone familiar with the routines of daily life in the school and community.

The following examples illustrate the kind of detailed questions—frequently overlooked—that should be asked by educators who have been offered an overseas contract:

Is the cost of owning and operating a car prohibitive?

What is the typical length of a lease for an apartment? Are one-year leases possible?

Are there any hidden costs in renting (deposits, utilities, etc.)?

Are textbooks and other instructional materials current?

If there is a medical program, am I covered immediately, or is there a waiting period?

As a teacher, will I be assigned any extra duties that are not stated in the contract?

Are there any restrictions on where I may live?

What was the biggest surprise you encountered when you first joined the staff?

Applicants should not be afraid to also ask a few minor questions about topics of special interest. J. Chris Anderson, a former teacher in Zaire, wishes that he had asked what the fishing was like before leaving for his assignment. Inquiring about topics that may seem trivial to others can sometimes make the difference between a tolerable and a pleasant overseas experience.

REACHING A DECISION

Experienced educators strongly suggest that the decision to accept or reject a contract for an overseas assignment should not be rushed into and that the pros and cons be carefully considered; emotion and excitement must not be allowed to interfere with clear, logical thinking. Compiling and analyzing a list of personal and professional considerations may help to eliminate or at least minimize emotional biases. The sample Considerations Chart on the facing page should serve as a useful starting point.

CONSIDERATIONS CHART

+	−	0	
			Salary
			Benefits
			Travel
			Security
			Prestige
			Leave of Absence
			Supplies and Equipment
			Commodities
			Family Separation
			Children
			Spouse
			Educational Advancement
			Continuing Higher Education
			Pleasant Working Conditions
			Intellectual Stimulation
			_____
			_____
			_____

After reviewing and modifying or expanding the considerations listed on the sample chart, educators should assign to each item a positive, negative, or neutral value. Putting down on paper the rationale for assigning the value is strongly recommended, both for subsequent reference and to promote honest, objective evaluation. To illustrate, let us examine six major considerations and assign hypothetical values to each.

+ *Salary*
The contract offer is at a salary less than my current income, but housing is provided, so that a net gain will result in cash for discretionary spending. Salary, then, becomes a plus.

0 *Family Separation*
The extended period of time away from my parents would be a difficult adjustment. They are in good health and are supportive of my desire to go abroad. Neither positive nor negative; evaluation is neutral.

− *Security*
Accepting an overseas contract would mean resigning from my current position, since I am not eligible for a leave of absence for two more years. I could not be assured of being rehired in this community. Negative.

+ *Travel*
Taking the position would afford opportunities for extensive travel at reasonable cost during holidays and vacations. Definitely a plus.

0 *Spouse*
My spouse says any decision I make will be acceptable. I sense a real attempt not to influence me to go or to stay. This has to be considered neutral.

+ *Educational Advancement*
The opportunity to conduct research in my field of specialization will be increased by the ease of access to original manuscripts in the host country. Publications based on this research should enhance my chances for promotion or will make me more marketable for a new position. Obviously a plus.

Once values have been assigned to each item, a tally of the positive, negative, and neutral considerations can be made. If the results are not conclusive, further examination of motivations, preferences, priorities, and considerations should be undertaken.

Because there is a great deal at stake for the applicant and all dependents, the decision to take an overseas position needs to be analyzed, calculated, pondered, and openly discussed with those whose lives will be affected. The applicant's spouse as well as older children who would accompany the educator may also find it useful if they each prepare their own individual Considerations Chart. A comparison of the values assigned to each item can serve as the basis for an open and honest family discussion.

WHAT'S IN A CONTRACT?

A contract is a legal document that outlines specific responsibilities and obligations agreed to by the educator and the employing institution. Educators who have completed application forms from several different international schools will not be surprised to learn that the contracts they receive may be exceedingly diverse in style and format. Some are relatively brief; others may fill several pages of fine print. Regardless of the length or appearance of the document, it must be read carefully to ensure an understanding of the terms and provisions outlined in the various clauses. Most contracts will contain clauses covering the items outlined below:

Acceptance

Nearly all contracts will provide specific instructions for returning the signed document, including a date by which the contract must be returned.

Dependents

Most contracts define authorized dependents as the educator's spouse and children—natural, adopted, or stepchildren—who are under the age of 18. Allowances or other benefits for dependents, where applicable, are restricted to the number of dependents listed in the contract, except that children born or adopted during the term of the contract automatically become authorized dependents.

Term of Contract

Although some schools require a minimum commitment of two years, the contract may be issued for only one year. If the contract is issued for more than one year, clauses covering salary, benefits, and travel expenses should reflect scheduled increases for the second year.

Duties

A part of the contract may outline in detail the educator's instructional and/or supervisory duties, but more often this clause merely specifies the job title and indicates the title of the person or persons responsible for assigning specific duties and evaluating performance.

Physical Examination

Many contracts contain a clause requiring a medical examination before the contract can become effective. A medical report may be required, to be returned along with the signed contract. If the employer is liable for the expense of a required physical examination, the amount of such liability and method of payment will be stipulated in the contract.

Place of Residence

Travel expenses and shipping allowances for the employee and authorized dependents are usually calculated from the educator's current place of residence. Return travel and shipping costs after the assignment has been completed are also calculated to this point.

Compensation and Benefits

The total compensation package will usually be itemized under some or all of the following categories:

a. Salary

The contract should explicitly state the annual salary and frequency of payment, along with the number of working days required. Deductions from salary due to absence from duty are usually on a prorated basis, determined by dividing the annual salary by the number of working days.

b. Housing

If housing is furnished by the employer, or a housing allowance is to be paid the employee, the contract should stipulate exact responsibilities of each party for maintenance, services, and utilities.

c. Travel

Allowances paid for the employee and authorized dependents to travel from the designated place of residence to the work site usually cover airfare and the cost of a stipulated amount of excess baggage. The contract may provide for advance payment or for reimbursement of expenses upon presentation of receipts. Sometimes a per diem allowance for the employee and dependents while in transit may be authorized. Provisions for return travel at the end of the commitment should also be described.

d. Shipping

The contract should specify allowances for shipment of the employee's and authorized dependents' personal belongings to and from the host country, including air freight and surface transportation.

e. Health Insurance

Employer contributions to the cost of health insurance premiums should be stated. Employees may be expected to pay the cost of premiums for family health insurance to cover authorized dependents. Major medical insurance is often a separate policy, and the employer may require employees to participate in a group plan or to provide evidence of equivalent private coverage.

f. Medical Evacuation

In the event that health problems make it impossible for the employee to fulfill the duties of the contract, the contract may provide for termination of the contract and return passage to the designated place of residence for the employee and authorized dependents. Some contracts further provide for payment of a portion of the employee's salary after termination of the contract.

g. Retirement Plans

Employer and employee contributions to a retirement plan, if applicable, may be outlined in the contract.

h. Tuition

The educator's children usually may attend classes at the employing institution at no charge. If the employing school does not provide instruction at the appropriate grade level, tuition may be provided for authorized dependents to attend another school.

i. Leaves

Provisions for an employee's accrual and use of sick leave should be specified in the contract. Midcontract and summer leave allowances as well as procedures for authorization of emergency leaves, personal leaves, and leaves without pay should also be outlined.

j. Local Transport

If the school furnishes a car or pays a car allowance, terms should be stated.

k. Rate of Exchange

If host-country laws permit deposit of a portion of the salary in a foreign bank, this option and the current rate of exchange may be stated in the contract; if the rate of exchange is subject to fluctuation, this will be noted.

Documentation of Education, Experience, and Certification

If copies of official transcripts, teaching or administrative certificates, or documents verifying work experience have not been submitted, the contract may contain a clause requiring that these items be returned with the signed contract. Many contracts include a statement to the effect that any statements furnished by the employee that are not true or valid will be considered grounds for termination of the contract.

Contract Renewal

The initial contract may include a clause outlining procedures for renewal and specifying dates for offer and acceptance of a renewal contract or extensions.

Termination

Procedures for voluntary termination or for involuntary termination for cause will be outlined and defined. Consequences of early termination and any compensation, advances, or allowances due the employee or subject to being reclaimed by the employer will be specified.

Overseas contracts can and do vary as much as stateside contracts. Some are written in clear, straightforward language easily understood by a general reader; others are considerably more complex, incorporating legalistic phrases and jargon. If points need clarification, the educator may contact the employer, or, to save time, an opinion may be sought from a local school official who is familiar with contract terminology. If there are discrepancies between the contract and the educator's expectations, the employer should be contacted immediately. Any discrepancies should be pointed out in writing, and a written response from the employer should be obtained before the contract is signed. If time does not permit the exchange of letters, the educator should telephone the employer for clarification and should confirm in writing any points discussed. Educators must remember that contracts are written not only for the benefit of the employer; they are designed for the mutual interests and protection of both parties. It is the educator's responsibility to understand the terms of the contract and to ensure that the rights and obligations set forth in the contract make the educator an equal partner in the educational process.

ACCEPTING OR DECLINING A CONTRACT

Although applicants may spend months waiting for a contract to be offered, there is no time to waste once a job offer has been received and a decision has been reached. When the educator has arrived at a decision to accept or reject a job offer, the employer must be informed of the decision as soon as possible. Depending upon previous communication and directives from the employer, the educator who has received the offer may cable or telephone a response or send a letter stating that the contract has been accepted or rejected. Writing this final letter confirming the decision is always to the educator's advantage and is a professional courtesy appreciated by all employers.

Educators should be certain that the employer receives the decision via air mail—or cable, if time is of the essence; an acceptance letter has little effect if it does not reach the employing official within the time period that has been specified. If a signed contract is to be returned by mail, it should always be accompanied by a cover letter stating that the document is enclosed. The letter should also confirm teaching assignments and state arrival plans, if known. If the decision to decline an offer is reached, it is not necessary to return the unsigned contract, but it is essential to write a letter to the hiring official stating that the contract offer will not be accepted. Depending upon the reasons for rejecting an offer, the educator may choose to be specific or to state in general terms that the contract is not being accepted.

In the two samples provided on the following pages, the first letter declines a contract offer, and the second letter confirms acceptance. These letters follow the same guidelines as all employment letters; they are typed in business style on standard bond or good-quality airmail-weight paper. As with all business correspondence, copies should be retained for the educator's file.

SAMPLE CONTRACT REFUSAL LETTER

```
                              12 Palm Drive
                              San Diego, California 92181
                              April 14, 1984


Norman J. Wesley, Director
The American School of Antananarivo
P.O. Box 1210
Antananarivo, Madagascar

Dear Mr. Wesley:

    After careful consideration, I must inform you that I am
not able to accept your April 7 contract offer to teach history
in The American School of Antananarivo.  I appreciated your
straightforward and detailed information about your students,
curriculum, and community and feel that I would have found
the position very rewarding but, because of the concerns and
priorities of my family, I must decline at this time.

    Thank you for the invitation to join your staff.  In the
event that my circumstances change in the future, I would be
very interested in talking with you again about employment
opportunities.

                              Sincerely,



                              Martin J. McCoy
```

SAMPLE CONTRACT ACCEPTANCE LETTER

21 Hawkeye Court
Hamilton, New York 13346
May 12, 1984

Professor Eibe Braun
Head, Department of Germanic Studies
University of Stuttgart
Keplerstrasse 7
D-7000 Stuttgart 1, Germany

Dear Dr. Braun:

I am sending this letter to confirm my acceptance of the two-year lecture and research appointment in your department which you offered to me during our telephone conversation on May 10. I wish to thank you for your confidence in selecting me for this prestigious faculty position and I want to assure you that I will fulfill the terms of the agreement.

The opportunity to return to Germany to continue my research and to share with your students and faculty my particular expertise in linguistics is anticipated with pleasure and excitement. I will look forward to receiving the official letter of appointment from you and Chancellor Marvin Schmidt in the near future.

My tentative plans are to arrive in Stuttgart during the week of August 20. I am quite familiar with the city, but your offer to assist me in locating housing close to campus is indeed appreciated. If questions should arise, please feel free to contact me either at my home or campus address.

Sincerely yours,

Doris Ann Hansen

Most people find it relatively easy to write a letter accepting a contract and to understand its necessity, but a letter that declines a contract offer is equally important. The letter must state explicitly what decision has been reached; there should be no question in the reader's mind about the decision.

Martin McCoy's letter states very clearly that he is declining the contract offer. Without going into specific detail, Martin states that his decision was based on the wishes and welfare of his family; he avoids being apologetic about his decision and maintains a positive tone.

Martin's letter is brief and to the point. The closing paragraph demonstrates his appreciation of the offer to join the staff and attempts to keep his future employment options open. He knows that international school administrators such as Norman Wesley enjoy working in various parts of the world, and their paths may cross again. Martin also understands that overseas administrators form a closely knit group and communicate frequently with each other. This administrator could be instrumental in recommending him for another position at some later date.

The contract acceptance letter written by Doris Hansen accomplishes three major objectives: it confirms her acceptance of the faculty appointment, shares her enthusiasm about the position, and clarifies dates and materials to be received. In the first paragraph, Doris confirms in writing points that were earlier discussed in a telephone conversation. To avoid any misunderstandings, Doris outlines the terms of the appointment by stating that it will be for two years, that it is a combination lecture and research appointment, and that the offer was received on May 10. The second paragraph illustrates that Doris is looking forward both personally and professionally to the position in Germany. She reminds Dr. Braun that she is anticipating an official letter of appointment. In conclusion, Doris gives her arrival dates and accepts Dr. Braun's offer to assist in locating appropriate housing.

While Doris's letter is brief, it covers all essential information. Most letters are written in English. In this case, because Doris is fluent in German and is accepting employment in a German university, she could have chosen to write in that language.

HONORING THE CONTRACT

A signed contract represents legal and ethical commitments to fulfill specific obligations. Except in the case of major and unforeseeable changes in the educator's circumstances—or significant alteration of conditions in the school or country of assignment—to back out of a contract for an overseas appointment is professionally and ethically irresponsible. Richard Chesley states that "too often teachers accept a contract or sign a contract assurance but later find reasons to back out. There are few things as disconcerting as a cable informing the administrator that a teacher is not coming in. Not only must replacements be located at an inconvenient time of the year, but also, a late start in preparing them to come in may delay their arrival until well after school has begun." Educators owe it to themselves and to their employers to learn as much as they can about the school and community in which they have sought employment. They should accept an offer only if they have every intention of fulfilling the terms of the contract.

Before I left I made a will, sold my furniture, purchased a new bicycle, held a garage sale, had dental work done, ordered additional pairs of glasses, got immunizations, bought lightweight clothes, recorded favorite music selections, and visited friends. I should have bought more clothes, more shoes and sandals, and more books for leisure reading.

Janice Guyer
Dhahran, Saudi Arabia

I should have known more about Eastern religions and cultures. I should especially have tried harder to know the Eastern mind.

Theodore G. Schweitzer III
Bangkok, Thailand

Getting a physical, a work permit, a visa, and a passport were my major concerns in preparing to come to Europe. Of course I bought clothes and shoes before coming over since I had heard they were quite expensive over here. I shipped five or six boxes of clothing. I wish I had learned French before coming over, but I didn't have time.

Gary Goodell
Brussels, Belgium

Stop using checks or credit cards at least thirty days in advance of your departure to ensure ample time for outstanding debts to be cleared. Secure the authorization of the local consulate to allow duty-free passage of all personal possessions into your employing country. Take a crash course in the language—every little bit helps. Write to your future school and ask for their "shopping list" of items not available within your future country.

Padric M. Piper
Belo Horizonte, Brazil

Bring along an extra sense of humor and three boxes of patience.

Ross L. Iverson
Tegucigalpa, Honduras

Chapter Six

Getting Ready

The interim between the signing of a contract with a foreign school and the first working day can be both exhilarating and exhausting. Sharing the news with colleagues, friends, and family, securing required documents, completing travel arrangements, and organizing personal possessions in anticipation of departure all will occupy much time and effort. In addition to the business of preparing to leave for the new assignment, educators should set aside time for acquiring or enhancing both language skills and knowledge of the culture of the country where they will be living for the next year or two. Although most educators have begun the process of learning about their host country prior to interviewing and accepting a contract, now that the overseas job has become a reality, intensive study may need to be undertaken. No educator has ever expressed regret about spending too much time learning the language, history, and culture of a new country, but many have lamented their ignorance upon arrival.

This chapter discusses the various steps to be taken in preparing to go abroad. Experienced educators who have traveled extensively can use the topics outlined in this chapter as a review; educators going abroad for the first time can treat the information as a useful starting point. Individuals may find it possible to bypass or combine some of the steps in the process of getting ready to leave for their new assignment, but each deserves careful consideration in order to ensure a smooth and pleasant predeparture experience.

LEARN THE LANGUAGE

Although English is spoken in many parts of the world, it is far from universal. Many monolingual Americans have good intentions of learning or at least obtaining a working knowledge of the language of the host country, but the flurry of activity involved in preparing to leave for a new assignment may leave little time for mastering a new language. Experienced educators have reported trying everything from do-it-yourself language manuals to private tutoring and crash courses at language institutes in the effort to acquire or enhance basic language skills. Educators invariably have found that any measures taken to become familiar with the language of the host country are well worth the time and expense. Charles West, who spent a sabbatical year as a Fulbright lecturer at the National Conservatory of Peru, reflects that his intensive language study was "the wisest preparation for Peru I could possibly have made."

GATHER CULTURAL INFORMATION

Gathering information about such basic things as population, topography, seasonal periods, annual rainfall, daily temperatures, and typical diets will reduce the chances for unpleasant surprises. Being familiar with available foodstuffs will give the relocated educator more confidence in shopping and in planning menus. Well-traveled people usually find that experimenting with unfamiliar foods can be an exciting experience; learning to substitute native foods for U.S. favorites can be accomplished with a little accommodation. As Michael D. Collins, a teacher in the Middle East, comments: "We've faced some dietary changes, since our favorite foods are not so readily available or affordable. For salads we now eat melon instead of lettuce, and we've learned to cook primarily with lamb instead of ham for our meat dishes."

ANTICIPATE CULTURAL DIFFERENCES

Recognition and acceptance of cultural differences will be easier for educators who understand that the "American way" is only one way. For example, it is important to realize that women's roles in some parts of the world are incompatible with the expectations of women in the United States, that certain hand and facial gestures have very different meanings in different parts of the world, and that initial greetings in some cultural settings may call for a physical embrace rather than a simple hello. As Philip Houseal wrote in his journal upon arriving in Peru: "The Latin culture has a closer distance physically, and I feel crowded. There is more touching and handshaking and kissing than Americans are comfortable with in social situations."

It is not easy, and, in fact, it may be nearly impossible, to ascertain from books the exact behaviors appropriate for the round of social situations one may encounter in a foreign environment. Talking with people who have lived in the area is by far the best way to learn about local customs and social expectations. If it is not possible to contact people with firsthand information before departure, then patience and observation will serve until local ways are understood.

START A JOURNAL

An organized approach to the many aspects of departure preparations can save the educator a great deal of time and emotional energy. One way to keep track of the multitude of tasks, arrangements, and related expenses (many of them tax-deductible) is to begin a journal. A journal may prove more efficient than a disjointed series of lists of "Things to Do." The habit of keeping a journal can be useful at this early stage and will prove to be a beneficial—and perhaps even amusing—record of events throughout the course of the overseas assignment. The journal need not be considered a diary; daily entries are not necessary, but all significant accomplishments and developments should be noted.

REVIEW COMMUNICATIONS

In the excitement of receiving and accepting a contract offer, small but important details are easily overlooked. This is the time to review the actual contract and all correspondence preceding or following it. Letters or cables received from or sent to the employer should be reviewed. In addition to refreshing one's memory about names of staff members or administrators with whom one is not yet acquainted, a thorough review of all communications may clarify dates, locations, and arrangements, and will diminish the chances for surprises and disappointments upon arrival. Suggestions for personal and work-related materials to ship ahead or to bring along should be checked again once the departure date is set and the time for packing approaches.

GET A PASSPORT

An essential step in preparing for departure is obtaining a passport—a government document certifying identity and citizenship—which is required for travel to nearly all foreign countries. The educator and each accompanying family member will be required to obtain a passport. Passports issued to adults are valid for ten years; individuals under eighteen years of age must renew their passports after five years. Because of possible delays in processing the passport application, educators and their family members who do not already have a valid passport should arrange to obtain and complete passport applications immediately after a contract has been accepted.

In order to obtain a passport, the following materials are required:
1. completed passport application form
2. proof of identity
3. proof of United States citizenship
4. two identical photographs of specified size
5. fee (currently $42 for the initial passport, $35 for renewal).

For complete information, contact a post office or a federal courthouse, or send a postcard to:

Office of Passport Services
U.S. Department of State
1425 K Street, N.W.
Washington, D.C. 20524.

VISAS AND WORK PERMITS

A visa is official permission granted by the government of a country to visit that country for a certain period of time. Before leaving the United States, educators going abroad should obtain any visas that will be needed during the assignment. A visa can be obtained in the United States by submitting (either by mail or in person) a valid passport along with a completed visa application form to the consular official of the foreign country requiring the visa. The majority of foreign consular offices in the United States are located in Washington, D.C., New York, Chicago, New Orleans, and San Francisco. It is recommended, and in some cases may be required, that the educator obtain a visa from the consular office closest to the educator's place of residence. Addresses of all foreign consulates may be obtained by consulting the *Congressional Directory,* available in most libraries. Visa requirements and regulations differ from country to country. For complete information, a pamphlet entitled "Visa Requirements of Foreign Governments" is available at any passport office or can be obtained from the Office of Passport Services in Washington, D.C.

In addition to passports and visas, work permits may also be required in order for United States citizens to be employed in some foreign countries. The employer generally will help to expedite the paperwork involved in obtaining work permits for new staff members or else will provide specific instructions for obtaining the required permits.

INTERNATIONAL DRIVER'S LICENSE

Obtaining an international driver's license is an optional though highly recommended step that educators can and should take care of before their departure. United States driver's licenses are not recognized in every country. In addition to allowing the individual to drive legally in most foreign countries, the international driver's license will serve as another form of identification. An international driver's license can be obtained at the local office of an established automobile association upon presentation of a valid U.S. driver's license together with two passport-sized photographs and payment of a small fee.

PERSONAL PAPERS AND FINANCES

In contrast with the relatively simple and straightforward paperwork for the passport and other required forms, paperwork dealing with more personal items will probably take considerable time and effort. For this reason, these matters should be dealt with well in advance of the departure date. A significant though often ignored document to be considered is a will. A family member, attorney, or other party in the United States should be informed of the existence and location of the will. This person might also be used as a stateside contact to assist in handling financial matters, mail, and other personal business that may arise in the educator's absence.

Personal financial matters must also be attended to before departure. Use of credit cards or charge accounts should be discontinued approximately two months before departure in order to be able to attend to any outstanding obligations. Depending upon individual situations and locations, it may be preferable to cancel accounts or memberships. While settling financial affairs, educators should obtain travelers' checks for last-minute departure and settling-in expenses. Employers are usually able to give an estimate of the amount of money required for relocation and settling-in expenses, but educators should be sure to take along adequate funds to tide them over until salary payments begin. Richard Chesley notes that "the first few months are usually financially difficult anywhere overseas. Laying in a stock of staples, purchasing and licensing a car, prepaying rent and utilities unless provided or supported by the school, and expending funds for incidental household items and other settling-in costs required in specific locations will constitute a heavy drain on personal savings. As a result, almost all teachers experience considerable financial pressure during the settling-in period."

Many experienced educators also suggest maintaining a stateside bank account to deposit a portion of monthly earnings for safekeeping and for use upon reentry to the United States. Some also maintain a stateside checking account for convenience in handling payment of taxes or other occasional expenses in the United States.

INSURANCE

The benefits package that employers offer to employees generally will include some form of medical and life insurance, but the educator must be aware that coverage provided by these policies may be limited. Some policies require a waiting period before employees are eligible for benefits; some may apply only while the employee is within the host country. The schedule of medical benefits may be based on comparable costs in the United States or may be determined according to local rates. Coverage in some policies may be limited to the educator and not extend to dependents. Educators should check the contract carefully to determine exactly what type of protection is provided. In some cases, they may find it necessary or preferable to retain or acquire supplementary insurance policies with U.S. companies in order to ensure adequate coverage for themselves and their dependents.

MEDICAL AND DENTAL CHECK-UP

Some employers require that new staff members submit the results of a medical examination prior to their arrival. If required, the employer generally will provide the necessary forms as well as any instructions for their completion and return. Depending upon the educator's relocation destination, vaccinations or inoculations may be required or advisable. Information pertaining to health requirements or precautions is routinely provided by employers. Even if a medical examination is not required, it is foolhardy for anyone to contemplate an extended stay outside the country without thorough medical and dental examinations. All medical or dental problems should be attended to well in advance of the date of departure.

PERSONAL POSSESSIONS

Deciding whether to store, sell, or otherwise dispose of personal possessions such as cars, furniture, appliances, and books will depend upon the anticipated length of employment overseas. An educator on a one-year leave of absence will plan quite differently from one who intends to be away from the United States for two years or more. Key factors to consider include:

- value and current marketability of the property
- maintenance needs
- storage facilities and expenses
- need for cash-in-hand

While in the process of organizing personal possessions, educators must keep in mind employer suggestions for items to be shipped to the new location and requirements for personal comfort. It is important not to be burdened with unnecessary personal and professional materials; on the other hand, taking along certain items that are personally meaningful is advisable in order to ease the transition and to make the stay comfortable.

PREPARING ACCOMPANYING DEPENDENTS

Although it is often true that children adjust easily and quickly to new and unfamiliar environments, educators going abroad should be aware that the amount of preparation required will depend upon the age of the children, the extent of their involvement in the decision-making process, the length of the commitment, and the degree of difference between the home setting and the new country. In general, it is wise to make children feel that they are participants in the predeparture stage of preparation for the move. Painting a clear picture of the move well in advance of the departure date and treating children as partners in a new adventure will be to everyone's advantage. Sharing the positive aspects of relocating without overinflating expectations will reduce the risk of a child feeling let down, betrayed, or deceived once the novelty wears off. It is also important to anticipate any aspects of the move that children are likely to view as negative, such as the absence of familiar faces or the unavailability of favorite foods and entertainments. To help offset any sense of loss they may experience, children should be encouraged to choose the valued personal possessions they would like to be shipped to their new home overseas, such as stuffed animals, roller skates, or favorite games and books.

Depending upon the age of the children, cultural information about the host country might be shared through pictures, books, and films. Taking the child along on trips to the library to look for new material can make the data-gathering more meaningful. Even young children should be encouraged to learn a few words or phrases of the language of the host country; if it can be arranged, older children may benefit from language study with a tutor.

REASSURING THOSE LEFT BEHIND

It is not unusual for family members and close friends to react cautiously or even negatively to an educator's announcement of a new position thousands of miles away from home. Emphasizing the reasons for making the decision to go abroad and the benefits to be gained both personally and professionally may make it easier for those left behind to accept the decision and to overcome feelings of loss or abandonment. In addition, it may help to reassure family members that communication will not be difficult, that contact can be maintained by telephone from virtually anywhere in the world, and that letters, tapes, and photographs can be exchanged regularly.

Extending invitations to visit in the new location, discussing the possibility of returning home on midcontract leave, and emphasizing that the contract is for a fixed term and not forever may be welcome notes of reassurance for loved ones. Some anxieties can be alleviated by providing family members with the name of the administrator in the new school and with the name of the stateside contact that has been chosen to handle the educator's personal affairs while overseas. If the family members have not traveled extensively, it is usually necessary to reassure them about personal safety and well-being. One way to do this might be to mention familiar companies doing business in the new location or to let family members know that churches, clubs, and other social organizations will be available as part of the overseas American community.

TELLING COLLEAGUES

Professional courtesy and common sense dictate that administrators be officially informed of an educator's decision to take a new position before the news is shared with colleagues while relaxing in the lounge or lunching in the cafeteria. In particular, details of sabbatical leave or resignation should be fully cleared with the administration before colleagues are informed. Although educators accepting an overseas assignment may find it difficult to conceal their enthusiasm and excitement about the new position, they should try not to overwhelm their colleagues or to dominate conversations with their new career plans while simultaneously ignoring the concerns of others. Educators should not expect to find their enthusiasm necessarily matched by their colleagues; they should be prepared for reactions ranging anywhere from a casual "That's very nice," or a hearty "Congratulations! Tell me all about it!" to assorted negatives such as "You'll miss your job and your friends when you give them up," or "I hope you make it back alive."

Reactions may not be as supportive as the educator would expect for a variety of reasons; envy, complacency, provincialism, naiveté, or any number of factors may prevent colleagues from sharing the educator's enthusiasm. Educators should remember that until they themselves became involved in the overseas job search they might have reacted to such news from a colleague in much the same way. Whatever the reactions of fellow staff members and in spite of the many details that must be attended to, it is essential to maintain a harmonious working relationship and to fulfill obligations to students, colleagues, and administrators for the balance of the school year. Leaving on a positive note will make it easier to return from a sabbatical as a valued team member. It is also conceivable that these same colleagues and administrators can be of assistance in a future stateside job search.

TRAVEL ITINERARY

Once departure and travel plans have been made, the educator should inform both the overseas administrator and the stateside contact of final arrangements by providing each with a complete and detailed itinerary. The itinerary should contain information regarding predeparture stateside travel, scheduled stopovers in foreign locations, flight numbers, hotel reservations, and names, addresses, and telephone numbers of friends and relatives. If unexpected circumstances should develop which would hamper or delay an educator's arrival plans, or if last-minute changes in assignment are necessary, the administrator will then be able to reach the educator by cable or telephone without significant delay. Even if exact details of the itinerary have not been finalized, both the stateside contact and the overseas administrator should be given each other's name, address, and telephone number.

ITINERARY FOR MELANIE HOLEN

July 15	Depart South Bend, Indiana
July 17	Arrive Atlanta, Georgia Visit parents: Ivend D. Holen 23 Maple Street Atlanta, Georgia 30303 (404) 658-2001
July 22	Depart Atlanta
July 24	Arrive New York City Parkview Hotel (212) 690-4335
July 28	Depart New York Kennedy Airport TWA Flight #627, 8:00 p.m.
July 29	Arrive Athens, Greece Stadium Hotel 21-4898
August 6	Depart Piraeus Anna Maria Cruise Line, 9:00 a.m.
August 10	Arrive Limossol, Cyprus, 2:00 p.m.

Copies to:

George Williamson
American Academy of Cyprus
P.O. Box 6735
Larnaca, Cyprus
37-2148

Maureen H. Smith
430 Terrace Avenue
South Bend, Indiana 46628
(219) 239-4663

PACKING

Deciding what to take along is never easy. Most people find it helpful and relatively simple to draw up a packing list. No matter how carefully packing is planned, however, a certain number of oversights or misjudgments are virtually inevitable, and hindsight is always clearer. Philip Houseal describes what may constitute a typical packing experience for the educator heading overseas: "I had to gather a 750-pound shipment of household and personal goods that would last the duration of my two-year contract. This included clothing, some appliances, reading and teaching materials, kitchen goods, instant foods, and hobby materials. In retrospect, I see that I took more than necessary. Peru offered more personal conveniences than I had been led to believe, and I found I could do without many of those that were unavailable. In other words, if I had it to do over, I would leave out, among other things, the two dozen rolls of Northern bathroom tissue and the ten boxes of Lipton's Cup O' Soup."

Before making a packing list, it is advisable to study carefully the weight limitations for shipped goods specified in the contract as well as the employer's recommendations and any suggestions gathered from people who are familiar with the school and the area. Educators will benefit by developing two separate lists, one for clothing and other personal items and one for professional materials.

The selection of professional materials to be shipped will be influenced by teaching style, classroom assignments, and materials available in the host country. The items listed below are examples of professional materials an elementary school teacher may wish to ship ahead.

PROFESSIONAL MATERIALS

finger puppets	tracing paper	puzzles
valentines	felt-tipped markers	games
holiday pin-ups	watercolors	tacks
transparencies	paintbrushes	tape
flash cards	coloring books	glue
textbooks	storybooks/songbooks	yarn
scissors	records/cassettes	
construction paper	musical instruments	

Careful planning and selection are essential in order that desired personal items remain within specified weight limitations. By prioritizing personal items in the four basic categories listed below, educators are more likely to be satisfied with their choices once the shipment arrives in the new setting.

1. Clothing
   Climate will obviously affect wardrobe choices. Experienced overseas educators recommend that new arrivals bring with them a complete, basic wardrobe rather than planning to purchase clothing or shoes on arrival.

2. Personal items
   Educators should be sure to take along an ample supply of any personal products that are required or strongly preferred (e.g., eye-care products, shampoos, lotions, etc.). American products may not be available in the new setting or, because of import duties, may be prohibitively expensive.

3. Leisure items
   Packing favorite leisure articles (e.g., knitting or needlepoint kits, playing cards, etc.) can make after-school hours and weekends more pleasant. Including materials for both individual and group enjoyment will provide greater options.

4. Hardware and appliances
   Simple appliances, electrical adapters, and small items useful for basic repairs should not be overlooked. A few small tools and accessories will save time and alleviate frustrations during the settling-in period.

PERSONAL AND HOUSEHOLD GOODS

Leisure Items

tape recorder/cassettes	paperbacks	needlepoint
transistor radio	cards/adult games	crossword puzzles
camera/film	sports gear	stationery

Clothing

shoes, sandals, boots	formal attire	sleepwear
nylons, athletic socks	underwear	outerwear
casual attire		

Personal Items

cosmetics	feminine supplies	sunglasses
medicines	soaps, shampoos	umbrella
toothpaste/brush	extra glasses/contacts	

Hardware

nails/screws	adapters	cooking utensils
tape/picture wire	batteries	travel clock
sewing kit	can opener	calculator

LAST-MINUTE THOUGHTS

Once the basic steps in preparing for departure have been completed, the typical educator is likely to finish details of last-minute packing with both a sigh of relief and a slight feeling of apprehension. Everything possible has been done to prepare for the new assignment, and now the educator, with fingers crossed, hopes that everything on the other end will go as planned: that shipments will arrive on schedule, that—just as the cable states—someone will be at the airport to meet the plane, and that all of this isn't just a dream. It is natural to have second thoughts during this predeparture phase of an overseas assignment. Educators need not feel alone and isolated if, at this point, they feel that taking on the overseas commitment may have been a mistake, and if only they could go back six months and start all over again, they surely would stay put in their safe stateside job. Most educators secretly, if not openly, express reservations and apprehensions after committing themselves to spend two years of their life in a foreign environment. Gilbert Fernandes, who spent two years teaching in South America while on leave from his stateside position, remembers the anxiety he experienced before departing for Peru: "I worried about making all the necessary arrangements before moving overseas (selling possessions—house, car, furniture, etc.); I worried about liking the school, the administration, and the people in general; I worried about being successful in my new job; I worried about my wife and girls adjusting to and enjoying life in the Third World; finally, I worried about being happy when returning to Iowa after my leave of absence."

In spite of the inevitable doubts and fears and the physical and emotional stress of saying good-bye to friends and family members, once educators board the plane they are likely to feel a keen sense of exhilaration now that the new experience has truly begun. The flight to the new location is usually characterized as a time of great anticipation but also a time of quiet reflection. Just as the plane is suspended in air, the traveler is suspended between the familiar and the unknown.

Teaching in a new culture is like entering a new life: around each corner is an entirely different experience. I have taught in Thailand, Iran, and now Switzerland, and it just keeps getting better.

Theodore G. Schweitzer III
Geneva, Switzerland

Go into the overseas assignment with a completely open mind, with toleration, and with curiosity, and wherever you go it will be a rewarding experience. Be willing to learn and be patient with yourself.

C. Patrick Hotle
Cairo, Egypt

Many Americans overseas tend to live within a right triangle, with lines stretching from home to work to the American club. They spend a great deal of time reminiscing about the glories of McDonald's hamburgers and comparing in-country frustrations. That is their own affair, of course, but it often makes adjusting and coping unnecessarily difficult.

Richard C. Chesley
Monrovia, Liberia

Some people travel, others sit at home. Some go out and meet the neighbors, others stay comfortably within the American environment.

Karen Leonard
Istanbul, Turkey

In the school setting, culture shock can often result when you suddenly discover that several of the children in the classroom do not speak English, or that some students are several years ahead in math and several years behind in reading. It often comes as a surprise that the services provided by a large central office staff in a stateside school are performed by the classroom teacher in an overseas school.

Kathleen L. Johns
Lisbon, Portugal

Chapter Seven

Arriving and Adjusting

The moment of arrival in a new country can be one of the most exciting yet one of the most anxious of an educator's life. Each location brings new sights, smells, customs, and languages, and not even seasoned globetrotters are exempt from surprises and adjustments. Inexperienced travelers, who may know the location only through travel posters or brochures, are sometimes disappointed to find that the actual on-site arrival does not measure up to their expectations; they may feel somehow deceived or betrayed if the beauty of the country or the novelty of the culture is not immediately apparent.

Arriving and adjusting to a new assignment, new community, and new country will be experienced differently by every educator. Accommodations that must be made for cultural and educational differences encountered during the settling-in period are stepping-stones to a successful international experience. Maintaining a sense of perspective and always keeping in mind the original motivations for going abroad will help the educator through initial problems that may occur. The accounts of experiences presented in this chapter should help first-timers to anticipate accommodations and adjustments that will be needed, to recognize and prepare for the inevitable frustrations and difficulties, and to enjoy their new and unfamiliar experiences as they occur—and not only in retrospect.

WELCOME TO YOUR NEW HOME

Philip Houseal has fond memories of his welcome to Ilo, Peru: "Everyone was generous. I was housed immediately and loaned all necessary housewares until my shipment arrived. People asked me into their homes and accepted me into their social spheres readily. I later discovered that in such relatively isolated areas any new arrival is anticipated and viewed as a fresh addition to the American camp."

Most administrators of international schools are very sensitive to the importance of a newcomer's arrival, and many take steps to prearrange housing, to organize tours of the city and countryside, to coordinate the efforts of returning teachers who have volunteered to serve as big brothers or big sisters, and to plan social gatherings with teachers, administrators, parents, and other members of the community. Milt Pavlina, Superintendent of the Escola Maria Imaculada in São Paulo, Brazil, describes the efforts of his administration and staff to assist newcomers: "We find and provide adequate housing as well as transportation to and from the school each working day. In addition, we request that new teachers come a couple of weeks early so that we can take them around the city and introduce them to everyday living situations—supermarkets, restaurants, and places of interest. We attempt to place new teachers with staff who have been with us for at least one school year. Finally, we explain the money situation, as well as the high inflation rate and how the local government attempts to cope with it, and we open bank accounts for each new staff member."

Although most international schools offer some degree of assistance to incoming staff members, the educator should be mentally prepared to assume responsibility for becoming oriented and to function independently in the event that assistance is limited. The ability to communicate in the language of the host country may make the difference between a miserable first few days or weeks and a relatively easy period of getting established. A little learning is indeed a dangerous thing—if language skills are minimal, educators should be sure that any arrangements they undertake on their own are later verified by someone who is fluent in the host-country language.

GETTING ACQUAINTED

As a part of the attraction to overseas employment, many educators eagerly anticipate the opportunity to become acquainted with host-country nationals. In practice, however, the pressures of daily living and work often may tend to isolate the educator within the American community. As Theodore G. Schweitzer III, who has taught in international schools in Iran and Thailand and now works for the United Nations in Switzerland, states: "In most international schools, the faculty lives in a little America." Reflecting on his past teaching assignment in Colombia, David Samore observes: "The American teachers tended to socialize primarily with one another; this was done more from necessity than anything else. As middle-class workers, we had to make do in a rigidly stratified society." In other circumstances, the extent of one's involvement with the wider community may be largely a matter of personal choice. C. Patrick Hotle, an educator teaching in Egypt, notes: "Egypt has so many Americans that it is easy to 'hide out' in an American enclave, if that is what you want, or to hurl yourself into the culture knowing you can always escape again." In any event, familiar faces and the camaraderie offered by fellow Americans may be especially welcome at the beginning of an assignment in a new location. As time passes and educators feel more comfortable in their new setting, they may also experience a growing interest in meeting and mingling with members of the host population.

Whether they remain within the American community or attempt to broaden their circle of contacts by getting to know people not connected with the school, all educators will benefit from the advice offered by Richard Chesley: "No matter where you go or how long you stay, keep in mind that you are a guest in the country. People who indulge in rancorous criticism and complain about the host country and its people display their ignorance and are offensive. Those who express political opinions critical of the host-country government are completely out of line and may find themselves in serious trouble. We Americans spend a good deal of time criticizing our own government. That is part of our national birthright and democratic prerogative; however, it is an interesting experience to observe an American citizen react to criticism aimed at the United States by a foreign national. The usual result is immediate and vehement flag-waving. Foreign nationals feel quite the same way about their own countries."

AFTER THE HONEYMOON

Typically, educators begin the overseas experience with a feeling of elation. The goal has been reached, the long waiting period is over, and one is finally entering a fascinating new environment filled with novelty and adventure. Moving into new accommodations, whether prearranged by the school or located independently by the individual, is typically an exciting step for the newly arrived educator. Meeting one's colleagues and students, exploring the community, and discovering shopping areas, cafes, and other sources of leisure entertainment all contribute to a sense of discovery and the feeling that one is launching a new and important era in one's career. It is natural and normal to romanticize the initial impression that one has been anticipating for so long. The customs, dress, and activities of the host-country nationals may be perceived as sophisticated and cosmopolitan or quaint and charming. Almost every educator experiences a kind of honeymoon period upon arrival, when expectations are high and negative aspects of the new environment are ignored or dismissed as insignificant.

Later, the initial elation may give way to a series of frustrations, as the educator attempts to establish routines in household and shopping chores and in daily classroom preparations, and as patterns emerge in social and personal relationships with members of the academic community. At this point, difficulties may also begin to surface as the phenomenon that anthropologists label culture shock makes its appearance. To a greater or lesser extent, the new environment and culture that initially seemed so fascinating may now be perceived as distant, puzzling, or perhaps even foolish.

In simple terms, culture shock refers to a feeling of disorientation arising from one's inability to comprehend the social and behavioral cues of the dominant culture. Many factors contribute to the degree of disorientation a newly relocated individual may experience. The nature of the disparities between one's home country and the host country, the extent of one's advance knowledge of the new environment, and one's ability to perceive and adjust to differences all may play a role.

Although the extent to which each person is affected may be dramatically different, all educators should be prepared to experience some degree of culture shock, which can manifest itself in a variety of emotional or physical responses. For many, culture shock is principally a matter of emotions; feelings of confusion, uncertainty, helplessness, detachment, or superiority are common reactions. Bruce R. Fehn, a teacher in Thessaloniki, Greece, describes a typical manifestation of the culture shock phenomenon: "It can take the form of a suspicion of the native population, as if they were out to fleece foreigners." Other common symptoms may include insomnia, irritability, unusual fatigue, or change in appetite.

PROFESSIONAL ADJUSTMENTS

The phenomenon of culture shock and its attendant symptoms are almost inevitable for educators just beginning an overseas assignment, but even highly experienced and well-traveled professionals are susceptible. Almost all educators anticipate that some adjustment to the new environment will be necessary, yet many are surprised and dismayed to discover that they are experiencing the emotional ups and downs that they tried so hard to avoid by weeks or even months of preparation and planning. Advance preparation will go only so far in helping people adjust to an unfamiliar climate and culture. Regardless of the intensity of preparation, no educator should be under the illusion that everything will go smoothly and pleasantly during the first few months. A variety of professional and personal adjustments will invariably be required of any educator during the transition period.

Adjustments for Elementary and Secondary School Teachers

In adjusting to an overseas teaching assignment, educators should expect to encounter certain situations that will directly affect teaching style. John Stiles, a teacher in Brussels, illustrates a common situation encountered by elementary and secondary school teachers in overseas schools: "Dealing with a variety of mother tongues is quite a challenge. I find that I must give longer amounts of time for tests and must spend a lot of time (much of it during free periods) to help students who don't speak English well." Fair warning was undoubtedly given during the interview and repeated in subsequent communications, but the reality of having a number of students who are unfamiliar with American curricula or whose English language skills are not yet fully developed can present teachers with special problems that must be dealt with.

Many educators have commented on the intense teacher-student relationships that are formed in foreign schools. In contrast to students in stateside schools, many students are very dependent on their teachers because of the limited academic or social activities available outside the school. Classes are generally small, allowing for closer interaction in the classroom. The educator's role in supervising extracurricular activities or field trips to other countries also promotes a tighter bond between students and teachers.

Teachers should also be prepared for a relatively high turnover rate in the classroom; students enter and leave at all times during the school year. Parents' occupations with embassies, military services, or corporations may necessitate frequent relocation, and David and Sharon Chojnacki, of the International School of Ouagadougou, Upper Volta, identify "the sense of impermanence in the overseas school and the foreign community" as a major factor contributing to "a lack of continuity."

Teaching style may also be affected by the types of materials and facilities available at the school. Because of financial constraints, shipping delays, or bureaucratic red tape that hampers orders or customs clearance on supplies, teachers often must face a lack of necessary supplies or a long waiting period before desired items and equipment can be obtained. Daniel Baker, a former teacher in Belize City, Belize, notes the unavailability overseas of many teaching aids that educators in the United States often come to depend upon and to take for granted, such as "good lab facilities, films, slides, overhead projectors, television, and other media to use as resources. Basically, I had a chalkboard and chalk. This makes teaching more difficult and certainly a challenge. It requires one to be more inventive."

Adjustments for Administrators

Like classroom teachers, administrators should expect to encounter some differences in the manner in which they will operate in an overseas environment. Many administrators in international schools have had prior overseas experience in some capacity, but each new situation will require unique accommodations. Perhaps one of the most striking differences between stateside and overseas administrative positions is the frequent lack of a large pool of peer administrators with whom to exchange ideas, air problems, or simply socialize. Although regional conferences are held in every part of the world, many administrators miss the stimulation of regular professional contact available in the United States. Also, in contrast to most stateside positions, the chief administrator is in some instances totally responsible for instructional programs and curricula as well as all financial aspects of school operations. Administrators accustomed to the services of support personnel, curriculum planners, and other in-service specialists may be initially uncomfortable in assuming the role of the educational leader for the entire school community. Richard Underwood advises administrators to be "ready to accept sole responsibility, for there is seldom any place to pass the buck."

Administrators share with their teaching staff the problems of student transfers in and out of the school during the year; receiving and processing student records or sending them on to the student's new school are routine but time-consuming tasks. In addition to the paperwork involved in welcoming a new student, administrators must spend time meeting the student and the student's parents and perhaps introducing them to the American community. Even in schools where enrollments are relatively stable, the administrator's responsibility for communicating with parents in the community may take on epic proportions. "Public relations demands interfacing with or relating to families from forty to fifty different countries," reports James Braunger, Principal at the Taipei American School in Taiwan.

The rate of staff turnover in international schools is typically greater than in American school districts. Whatever the rate of turnover may be, the amount of time involved in hiring and orienting new staff members far exceeds the amount of time usually spent on these tasks in United States schools. In contrast to their stateside counterparts, overseas administrators may be much more involved in orienting new staff members not only to the school but to the larger community. In addition to their day-to-day administrative responsibilities, many overseas administrators function as welcoming committee, host, and tour guide for new arrivals. Adjustments must be made in personal and family schedules to accommodate the responsibilities of meeting new staff members after school hours, on weekends, and even sometimes during holiday periods.

Almost all overseas administrators comment on the frustrations encountered in dealing with unfamiliar bureaucratic red tape and the idiosyncrasies of local governments. Adjusting to the local way of doing things is essential. In order to succeed or even survive, administrators often must learn to cope with slow and inefficient communications systems and complicated procedures for obtaining customs clearance for supplies and materials being imported as well as clearances and work permits for new staff members.

Finally, although any experienced administrator has been involved with contingency plans for school or local emergencies, the overseas administrator must be able to assume the responsibility of implementing evacuation plans for students and teachers in the event of terrorist acts or political or military uprisings. Procedures for immediate action need to be established and reviewed regularly with local officials and United States military or embassy personnel.

Adjustments for College Professors

The professional adjustments required of educators working in college or university settings abroad are likely to vary depending upon the nature of the position or the anticipated length of the commitment. For example, an educator who has accepted a research fellowship or a short, fixed-term teaching appointment will generally be less involved with the inner workings of the university than one who has accepted a permanent, full-time appointment.

Regardless of the nature of the appointment, professors need to be aware that differences exist between a typical institution of higher education in the United States and an overseas university. Students usually represent a number of different nationalities, and expectations educators may have of student efforts, participation, and conduct may be quite different from their expectations of students in the United States. In some institutions grades may not be assigned, class attendance may not be required, and examinations may be optional; at the same time, however, more student contact may be required of the educator than is typical in many American universities. Educators may also have to adapt to limited English skills in both students and colleagues.

Unlike elementary and secondary school teachers employed in many international schools, the college professor is generally unlikely to have a large number of colleagues from the United States. Without day-to-day contact with American colleagues, college-level educators typically become more immersed in the culture of the host country; at the same time, however, foreign colleagues may tend to keep their distance because of differences in cultural and educational background. Alfrieta Parks Monagan, an anthropologist with teaching and research experience in a number of overseas areas, found that in most of her international assignments: "I was the visitor or foreigner who was coming to grips with 'the other,' and everyone interacted with me on those terms." Based on her experience as professor at the Kuring-gai College of Advanced Education in Sydney, Australia, Barbara Poston Anderson warns of another common adjustment that educators working abroad may face—a tendency to have to "prove" yourself all over again in the new environment.

A difference mentioned by many college professors is the greater status they enjoy because of the value placed upon education in most foreign countries. Based on her experience in Europe, the West Indies, and South Asia, Alfrieta Parks Monagan comments: "University instructors and those with higher degrees are held in higher respect and treated more formally than in the United States. For example, my students in Germany found it difficult to address me by my first name, and they were ill at ease with me in informal situations. Likewise, there was more formality among faculty members in Germany."

Gary Theisen, a Ford Foundation professor at the University of Indonesia, has found "more responsibility, independence, and authority in an overseas institution, with fewer meaningless committee meetings." In contrast to his stateside teaching experiences, Scott McNabb observes that working at Thammasat University in Bangkok, Thailand, offered "more flexibility in creating my teaching assignment—what classes I'd teach and what materials I'd use." Educators pursuing research in other countries are often surprised to discover how deeply involved they become in their projects. Alfrieta Parks Monagan reflects: "Research abroad is more intense than it is in your own country because you are removed from the everyday concerns of home, work, neighborhood, etc. You are essentially working most or all of the time."

PERSONAL ADJUSTMENTS

In conjunction with professional accommodations, educators at all levels should expect to make a variety of adjustments in their personal lives upon relocation in the foreign community. For example, they must be prepared to deal with unfamiliar currencies and, in some cases, vastly different methods of conducting financial or business transactions. Each location will present unique situations, necessitating adjustments and adaptations. Some of the major changes confronting educators working abroad may involve any or all of the areas discussed below.

Change of Climate

Major adjustments in daily routines and activities may be required in locations having extreme temperatures. Michael Collins has noted that his greatest shock upon relocating from the United States to Saudi Arabia was the temperature change and the effects it had both physically and mentally. Until one adjusts to the new climate, extreme heat or humidity can be enervating and exhausting. Educators in other locations have commented on the adverse physiological and psychological effects that may result in areas that are constantly cloudy, rainy, dark, or cold. The widespread stateside dependence upon central heating and cooling systems does not extend to the rest of the world. As Bruce R. Fehn comments from Thessaloniki, Greece: "There are physical adjustments that Americans employed overseas must be prepared to make. It's cold in Greece in winter, and the heating systems are not always satisfactory."

Daily Living

Educators who go abroad, especially for the first time, usually find everyday activities to be more complex and time-consuming than they were at home.

Gilbert Fernandes advises new arrivals to recognize that the first six months will be the most difficult: "Expect the simplest thing you do in the States, like going to the grocery store, to seem like a major problem until you become adjusted." Because American-style supermarkets are nonexistent in many parts of the world, daily shopping can literally take hours of time. In many countries, it is still common to go to individual shops or outdoor markets for meat, bread, and vegetables. Food preparation can also be a lengthy process; many prepackaged or convenience foods are uniquely American.

Appliances and household gadgets are so commonplace in the United States that most people take them for granted. Because of limited resources, often extending to both water and electricity, appliances may not be as readily available in many countries. The inconvenience of not having ready access to a washer and dryer may require some adjustment, for example. Karen Leonard, who has lived in Korea and Turkey, probably speaks for most international educators when she says: "I spend more time 'living' in a foreign country. Cooking, buying food, and taking public transportation all take considerably longer."

Communications

The scarcity and inefficiency of postal and telephone services in some parts of the world may be a major source of inconvenience for overseas Americans. In some locations, there may be a long waiting period before a telephone can be obtained, and a substantial deposit may be required. Robert Werner, while in Yaounde, Cameroon, found it necessary to adjust to the fact that because of poor mail service, it usually took a full month for him to receive mail from home.

Educators accustomed to starting their day with a morning newspaper may find it difficult to rely on late-arriving subscriptions to U.S. news magazines or English-language newspapers for their news coverage. Although available in most metropolitan areas, such periodicals may be difficult or impossible to obtain in remote locations. Adjustments may also be needed in the area of television viewing, whether for news or entertainment. Not only is television programming exceedingly limited in many countries, but educators may find that the expense of purchasing a television, which may be heavily taxed as a luxury item, is prohibitive.

Services

Few educators in the United States are accustomed to full-time domestic help, but in some parts of the world educators will find that local economic conditions allow them to employ housekeepers at surprisingly moderate cost. Holly Tancred, a teacher in Rabat, Morocco, writes: "As a working woman, I truly appreciate having a maid. Coming home to a clean house, clean clothes, and prepared food is an absolute delight." Ross L. Iverson, a teacher in Tegucigalpa,

Honduras, offers this comment: "Our maid gets the equivalent of fifty dollars a month for working eleven hours a day, six days a week. That will never make sense to me."

Regarding other types of services, educators living abroad should be prepared for the frustrations of time delays and broken promises involving repair or maintenance work. Though patterns of performance in this area obviously vary greatly in any location, in some parts of the world workers not showing up on time or work not being completed is a common occurrence. James Newmann shares a frustrating experience from his assignment in Lima, Peru: "Trying to get a copy of my front door key, I have gone to six different locksmiths; each time the key hasn't worked and the sixth guy also ruined the original."

Restrictions

Many Americans are unfamiliar with the existence in some parts of the world of legal or religious restrictions governing many personal liberties or day-to-day activities that U.S. citizens take for granted. Even though educators going abroad may have some advance knowledge of such restrictions, observing or actually encountering them firsthand can be a frustrating experience. As a teacher traveling in Saudi Arabia, Janice Guyer reported that her hotel reservations were cancelled when the hotel where she was to stay realized that she was a single woman. In some parts of the world, men and women are not permitted to socialize in clubs, in bars, or on public beaches. Some foreign governments place restrictions on the areas where foreigners are allowed to live or where they may travel and on books or other printed materials brought into the country.

Daily schedules may also be affected by legally or culturally imposed restrictions. Michael D. Collins, a teacher at the ARAMCO Schools in Dhahran, Saudi Arabia, writes that "it was an adjustment learning to plan all daily activities around the Muslim prayer times, since all shops and businesses close during prayer hours." Even if religious custom does not necessarily restrict business hours, many countries in hot climates follow the practice of closing shops and businesses during the early afternoon hours and reopening only in the late afternoon.

FAMILY ADJUSTMENTS

The impact of an overseas relocation will affect each member of an educator's family differently. Very young children usually adjust quickly to the new setting. Older dependents may find it much harder to leave behind their friends and familiar stateside extracurricular activities, although children who have actively participated in talking about and planning for their overseas experience will probably encounter fewer difficulties. A nonteaching spouse is in many cases the family member who encounters the greatest adjustment difficulties in an overseas move. Shirley Fernandes, who accompanied her teacher husband to Peru, writes: "Although my husband and daughters were very understanding, the lack of my usual activities and friends and my inability to speak Spanish made the first few months very unhappy, trying, and frustrating."

The settling-in period is typically a hectic time for the nonworking spouse. Unpacking, shopping, and helping family members prepare for the opening of school take up a good portion of each day. Once school begins, however, the nonworking spouse may feel isolated and abandoned. Furthermore, not yet having established a wide circle of friends, the spouse must depend upon the family for support and understanding, but the educator and dependent children are usually preoccupied with their own adjustments as they settle into their daily routines. In many countries it is difficult or impossible for the accompanying spouse to obtain a work permit. The combination of enforced idleness, loneliness, and unfamiliar surroundings can produce serious adjustment problems. To help ease these problems, inquiries about support groups and activities for nonemployed spouses should be made before leaving the United States. Advance knowledge can help the family make immediate contacts and thereby help spouses adjust to their new role in the foreign environment.

COPING STRATEGIES

Recognition of the culture shock syndrome and conscious efforts to develop coping strategies will help educators and their dependents deal with and adjust to the emotional and physical reactions brought about by an overseas relocation. The passing of time and increasing familiarity with the new environment will usually alleviate the ill effects of culture shock; however, there are immediate steps that can be taken to assist in reducing some of the tensions and frustrations.

Pampering

A simple but often effective remedy for sagging morale is to indulge in a little self-pampering. Taking or making time to engage in a preferred leisure activity, calling a friend or family member back in the States, treating oneself to a shopping spree, or simply splurging on an elaborate meal or favorite dessert can provide a short-term boost. While self-pampering will not provide long-lasting solutions to culture shock, it can temper depression and help one get through an emotional slump.

Writing It Down

A journal, which can be started before leaving the United States, can be an effective outlet for pent-up frustrations. The act of recording the irritations and feelings of loneliness, self-doubt, or anger will help to place the problems in perspective—especially if one also looks back at earlier entries and rediscovers the initial excitement and sense of anticipation.

Sharing Feelings

Another coping technique is to attempt to concentrate on helping others— whether family members, friends, colleagues, or students. Educators should be aware of and sensitive to the fact that many of their pupils may also be undergoing culture shock, either because they have recently relocated or because they are not fully accustomed to an American curriculum. Taking extra time to talk with and explore the feelings of such individuals may help to ease adjustments for both parties. Sharing one's own feelings with fellow faculty members also can be reassuring. Established staff members know from experience that culture shock during the adjustment period is natural and to be expected, and that discussing problems openly with others can lead to solutions.

UNDERSTANDING AND ACCEPTING

The amount of time that elapses from the moment of arrival until one is fully acclimated and able to function comfortably in the new environment cannot be determined precisely, but as Kathleen L. Johns, Principal of the American International School in Lisbon, suggests: "The first three to four months of any overseas experience are a time of discovery which often leads to frustration. Going to three different stores to try to buy a can opener, not being able to express yourself in the foreign language, and telephones that do not work are examples of minor setbacks which may lead to temporary culture shock. All of these are eventually overcome by a personality capable of being flexible, adaptable, and willing to accept that there are cultural priorities in every country."

Teachers and administrators who have remained in the overseas circuit recognize and understand the benefits to be gained from experiencing cultural and ideological differences. A successful experience may well depend upon the educator's ability to suspend, at least temporarily, the belief that the American way is more efficient, more just, or morally superior. As Thomas Rushcamp advises: "There are reasons why our host country does things in their way, and life would be so much easier if those of us who are guests would learn this early in our stay." From their experiences in four different overseas assignments, Lyn and Howard Collins offer insights that are relevant for any professional who is planning to go abroad. Lyn shares these thoughts: "We're not here to change the culture, only to offer the benefit of our varied experiences and education. We must learn as well as teach." Howard further recommends: "Expect things to be different, but take time to enjoy these differences. Don't try to change things, but be accepting of what is."

Expect a period of adjustment when you feel more at home "over there" than in the United States. Don't expect real interest in your experience except from close friends, and don't expect those who haven't had in-depth foreign experiences to ask penetrating questions. Celebrate the times you can truly share your foreign experiences.

Scott F. McNabb
Bangkok, Thailand

Upon each reentry, I have felt torn (a part of me here, another in the foreign country) and displaced. There is usually an eagerness to return to this country followed initially by a reluctance to be here because my behavior and feelings have become so geared toward those of the other country. My attitude is usually more critical toward behavior, customs, and values that I took for granted before my departure.

Alfrieta Parks Monagan
St. Augustine, Trinidad

I would have to describe my reentry experience as numbing and tinged with an odd feeling of vagueness. While the surroundings were familiar, the change from Colombia was so dramatic that it all seemed dreamlike.

David Samore
Barranquilla, Colombia

I think perhaps a reentry into American life was more difficult for me than adapting to the rural, so-called primitive life-style of natives in Zaire. I was deathly afraid of automobiles because they seemed to go so fast, and I was taken aback by how much our lives are cluttered by advertising.

J. Chris Anderson
Bulape, Zaire

Chapter Eight

Coming Home

Although some educators use their first overseas job as a stepping-stone to an international career, many teachers and administrators return to the United States after completing one or two foreign assignments. The decision to come home may be as complex and multifaceted as the decision to go abroad; both personal and professional goals must be considered. Strong family ties, concern for the spouse's career and the dependents' education, health and financial matters, or concern for personal safety due to changes in the political situation of the host country—these and other personal factors may motivate educators to return. The desire for greater job security and more or better fringe benefits (retirement plans, health coverage, etc.) can also influence the reentry decision. Professional reasons to return may include plans for career advancement or change, continuing education, or professional development. John E. Dansdill, a school administrator working in Peru, recommends that educators should "either plan on staying in overseas teaching for career purposes or spend two to four years and then return to the States, the mainstream of education."

Whatever the individual motivations for returning, all educators employed overseas, except those who were granted a leave of absence from a stateside position, will face the difficult task of finding a new job at long distance. The prospects for finding suitable employment can be disheartening for educators living out of the country. Planning for reentry requires as much effort as the initial overseas job search but usually lacks the excitement and spirit of adventure that characterized the overseas application process. Preparations for a smooth transition need to begin well in advance of the educator's return to the United States. Awareness of effective strategies and techniques must be refreshed and modified for the reentry campaign. Many educators delay their stateside job search because of the obstacles they anticipate but, in reality, the job search will be very similar to the one conducted for an overseas position. The major difference is the personal interview which, almost without exception, will be required at the school district, necessitating an on-site visit.

UPDATING PLACEMENT FILES

College placement offices or private placement agencies can provide optimal service if they are contacted early—ideally, six to eight months before an anticipated return. Updating the placement file so that current information will be readily available to prospective employers may take several weeks or even months depending on mail service. Current references from overseas administrators and/or supervisors will be an important component of the placement file. Just as an overseas administrator evaluated references in the screening process, so will stateside employers expect to have recommendations from the most recent teaching or administrative experience. Recommendations may be added to placement files or the applicant's personal file but should be obtained during the term of employment. Administrators, like teachers, may move from one position to another, and obtaining a recommendation after returning to the United States may prove difficult and frustrating if the administrator has moved and mail must be forwarded to another overseas address or back to the United States.

FINDING VACANCIES

Information about specific vacancies may be obtained from a number of sources. Many college placement offices and private agencies compile lists of vacancies reported to them. Educators who are registered with placement services should inquire about the availability of such listings. In addition to notices of specific openings, the listings may also contain information about summer job fairs for stateside positions as well as general advice about the current job market.

The classified sections of some metropolitan newspapers carry advertisements for positions in education. Practices regarding newspaper ads for teaching and administrative positions vary in different parts of the country. Educators interested in the Midwest, for example, will find literally hundreds of positions advertised in Iowa's *Des Moines Register*. The education section of the Sunday *New York Times* can be especially helpful for educators seeking college-level positions or those who are interested in private preparatory and boarding schools. Stateside contacts may be able to offer assistance in checking local newspapers for job-related information.

Professional publications should also be consulted by the job seeker. Announcements of administrative positions in elementary and secondary schools can be found in *Education Week,* the *Executive Educator,* and *Independent School.* A major source of vacancy notices for college-level teaching and administrative positions is the *Chronicle of Higher Education.* In addition, each academic discipline publishes professional journals and newsletters, many of which contain information about staff openings.

Educators who are interested in a particular geographic location will make their reentry campaign easier and more productive by writing letters of inquiry to potential employers. Many international schools maintain for their staff a professional library, which may include annual or periodic directories of public and private schools in the United States. Job seekers will find the following two standard reference works useful for obtaining names, addresses, and other relevant data: the *Directory of Public School Systems in the U.S.*, published by the Association for School, College and University Staffing, Box 4411, Madison, Wisconsin 53711; and *Peterson's Annual Guide to Independent Secondary Schools*, published by Peterson's Guides, Inc., P.O. Box 2123, Princeton, New Jersey 08540. Annually updated directories of public and/or private schools are also compiled by each of the fifty states. Directories are generally available for purchase from the department of public instruction located in the state capital. Addresses for individual state education offices are listed in the Appendix.

Educators seeking college-level teaching, research, or administrative positions should direct letters of inquiry to department heads. Most professional associations in higher education publish a membership directory that provides names and addresses of appropriate personnel. For general information about colleges and universities, educators should consult the Appendix for publication information about college-related directories.

PREPARING REENTRY PAPERWORK

As in any job search, it is imperative that cover letters and résumés present a positive professional image. Most educators will find it a simple matter to update and adapt their overseas résumé for a reentry job search. For purposes of illustration, on the following pages the overseas résumés of Stephen Nagel and Veronica George have been modified for reentry. A sample cover letter presented after each résumé demonstrates effective ways of relating the overseas experience to stateside situations.

STEPHEN NAGEL

Germany Address:

Karamursel American Elementary School
APO New York, New York 09086
(404-960, home phone)

Stateside Address:

300 4th Avenue
Kirkwood, Delaware 19708
(302-763-2021, parents' phone)

────────────────TEACHING EXPERIENCE────────────────

1970 - 1972	Seaford Elementary School, Seaford, Delaware. 3rd grade traditional, self-contained classroom.
1972 - 1978	Westwinds Alternative Elementary School, Dade County System, Miami, Florida. 2nd grade, team teaching, open-space classroom.
1978 - 1982	Custer Elementary School, Bismarck, North Dakota. 4th and 5th grade combination classroom.
1982 - present	Karamursel American Elementary School, Karlsruhe, Germany (Department of Defense Dependents School). 3rd and 4th grade departmentalized classroom. Presented the Outstanding Teacher Award, U.S. Army - Europe, 1983.

────────────────COACHING EXPERIENCE────────────────

1975 - 1978	YMCA boys' basketball club coach, Miami.
1979 - 1981	Summer baseball coach, Bismarck.
1982 - present	Soccer coach and intramural director, grades 1-7, Karlsruhe.
1983 - present	USAID summer recreation director, Karlsruhe and Stuttgart.
	Qualified to coach all boys' and girls' sports.

────────────────CERTIFICATION────────────────

North Dakota (K-9)   Delaware (K-8)   Florida Permanent (K-8)

────────────────INTERESTS────────────────

Outdoor interests include gardening, camping, sports, and traveling.

Youth group involvement includes extracurricular school programs, coaching, and Boy Scouts (Eagle Scout, 1964).

────────────────EDUCATION────────────────

1966 - 1970	Delaware State College B.S., Elementary Education	Dover, Delaware
1975 - 1977 Summer Sessions	University of Miami Reading endorsement	Coral Gables, Florida

────────────────REFERENCES AVAILABLE UPON REQUEST────────────────

Coming Home

Karamursel American Elementary School
APO New York, New York 09086
February 7, 1984

Susan L. Sundberg
Personnel Services
New Castle County School District
1400 Washington Street
P.O. Box 689
Wilmington, Delaware 19899

Dear Ms. Sundberg:

In June I will be returning to northern Delaware, and I am now in the process of exploring teaching and coaching possibilities in the Wilmington area. After graduating from Delaware State College, I started my teaching career in Seaford. Since then, my teaching experiences have taken me to Florida, to North Dakota, and to Germany, where I have spent the past four years.

The Karamursel American Elementary School, a Department of Defense Dependents School, is a typical U.S. elementary school with an active extracurricular program. As the enclosed résumé notes, I have been involved in coaching, intramurals, and recreation activities and would like to continue these interests.

If staff openings should exist at the elementary or middle school level, I would like to receive application materials in the enclosed self-addressed stamped envelope. During the month of June we will be visiting my parents in Kirkwood, and I would be interested in talking with you at that time about available positions.

Sincerely,

Stephen Nagel

Encs.

Stephen Nagel has chosen to use the same basic design for his reentry résumé that he used for his overseas résumé (see page 40). It is simple, straightforward, and easy to follow. Stephen begins by listing his current address in Germany and a United States address. Because Stephen is now interested in returning to the area in which he grew up, using his parents' address as a stateside contact emphasizes his ties to the area and provides the employer with a local contact.

By using the same chronological format, Stephen needs only to add the Karlsruhe, Germany, teaching position in the TEACHING EXPERIENCE category. He identifies the length of the experience, the name and place of the school, and grade levels taught. Since the name of the elementary school does not indicate that it is a Department of Defense Dependents school, Stephen has added this information for clarification. He included his Outstanding Teacher Award in this category because he did not want to exceed one page and he did not want to create a new category for this one item. Except for the addition of his current extracurricular involvement, the coaching experience section remains the same. In an effort not to duplicate information contained in the experience section, only the names of the cities have been listed in this category.

All three state certifications are listed in order to demonstrate that Stephen is qualified to work in elementary schools, middle schools, and junior high schools.

Stephen knows that the FAMILY INFORMATION category he had included on his overseas résumé is neither necessary nor appropriate for his stateside résumé, so he has replaced this section with an INTERESTS category to emphasize his strengths as a well-rounded individual. This information not only tells employers of Stephen's personal interests but reemphasizes his willingness to be involved with extracurricular and youth group programs. If his wife, Jane, decides to pursue teaching opportunities, she will submit her own résumé and cover letter independently.

Stephen's letter of inquiry establishes contact with prospective employers and requests application materials. The letter informs prospective employers that he has taught and supervised a variety of extracurricular activities in four different locations. He refers the reader to the enclosed résumé for more details. Although Stephen can expect employers to be familiar with U.S. Department of Defense Dependents schools abroad, he briefly emphasizes the fact that the Karamusel school is an Army-base school offering a curriculum comparable to U.S. suburban schools.

The final paragraph contains three essential pieces of information. In it Stephen states the specific teaching areas in which he is interested (elementary and middle schools); he encloses a self-addressed, stamped envelope for the employer's reply; and he informs the reader that he will be available for an interview upon his return to the area.

Coming Home

VERONICA R. GEORGE

Addresses: 14 Airway Drive   American School of Quito
            Tempe, Arizona 85283   P.O. Box 150
            (602) 839-2212 (summer)   Quito, Ecuador
                                      230-234 (office)

PROFESSIONAL BACKGROUND

Administration:

Secondary Principal, American School of Quito, Quito, Ecuador, 1983–present. Current leadership responsibilities include strengthening and developing the U.S.-based curriculum, budget preparation, public relations, and supervision of the American-trained teaching and administrative staff of 70 professionals and 750 students, grades 9-12.

Middle School Principal, Carson Middle School, Mesa, Arizona, 1981–1983. Responsible for administration of a staff of 28 teachers; bilingual multicultural student body of 420.

Assistant Principal, McClintock High School, Tempe, Arizona, 1979–1981. Responsible for discipline, attendance, behavioral conferences and class and staff scheduling.

Counseling/Teaching:

Head Counselor, Grand River Academy, Austintown, Ohio, 1975–1978.

Counselor/Family Living Teacher, 1972–1975, and Home Economics Teacher, 1969–1971, Grant Junior High School, Portsmouth, Ohio.

CERTIFICATIONS

Arizona Administration Certificate – Principal and Superintendent
Ohio Permanent Certificate – School Counseling
Ohio Permanent High School Certificate – Home Economics & Family Life Education

ACADEMIC TRAINING

University of Arizona 1978 - 1979 Ed.S. Educational Administration
Tucson, Arizona   1971 - 1972 M.A.   Counseling

Marian College   1965 - 1969 B.S.   Home Economics &
Indianapolis, Indiana   Family Studies

LANGUAGE & TRAVEL

Bilingual - Spanish/English
Traveled extensively in the continental U.S.A., Mexico, Central and South America.

REFERENCES

Peter Jones, Superintendent, Mesa USD #4 (647) 213-7904
Joseph Paul, Principal, McClintock High School (647) 112-7654
Rhea Adams, Director, Grand River Academy (419) 671-4646
Denise Schultz, Dean, College of Education, University of Arizona (602) 887-8765
Andreas Marino, Head, American School of Quito, 230-234

    Credentials including references available from Placement Service, R. L. Nugent Building #40, University of Arizona, Tucson, Arizona 85721 (602) 626-1232

147

PROFESSIONAL ACTIVITIES OF
VERONICA R. GEORGE

ACADEMIC SERVICE

Conference presentations:
Cross-cultural Curricula, Regional Conference of the American Schools of South America, Cordoba, Argentina.

Bilingual Education in the Southwest, Tri-State Principal's Conference, Albuquerque, New Mexico, 1979.

Counseling the Gifted, Midwest Counseling Conference, Columbus, Ohio, 1975.

Community involvement:
Co-chair, Citizen's Advisory Committee to the Superintendent, Mesa, Arizona, 1981.

Member, University of Arizona Committee for Friends of Foreign Students, Tucson, Arizona, 1978 - 1979.

Officer, Mahoning County Youth Services Bureau, Youngstown, Ohio, 1976 - 1978.

Numerous talks to college classes and civic groups, 1976 - present.

CURRICULA AND SCHOOL-RELATED PROGRAMS

Initiated and secured state and national monies for special learning programs in bilingual, gifted, and career education.

Designed school-wide counseling program involving counselors, administrators, classroom teachers, students and parents.

Started and encouraged the Parent/Teacher/Student Organization (PTSO) luncheon meeting.

Led visitation team, South Central Association, Houston Public Schools, Houston, Texas, 1980.

Developed the monthly faculty "Communicator."

Established all-school morning co-ed intramural program.

Evaluated certified staff member on a semester basis.

Organized regular teacher inservice training sessions.

Participated in school-wide budget preparations.

PUBLICATIONS

"Curriculum Creativity in Overseas Schools," Inter-Ed, The Association for the Advancement of International Education, Fall, 1983.
"Discipline in Decline," The Executive Educator, November, 1981.
"Counseling the College Bound Student," Psychology Today, March, 1977.

MEMBERSHIPS

National Association of Secondary School Principals
American School Counselors Association
Phi Delta Kappa
Association of American Schools of South America
The Association for the Advancement of International Education

Coming Home

American School of Quito
P.O. Box 150
Quito, Ecuador
March 24, 1984

Dr. Robert Vallejo
Assistant Superintendent, Personnel
Houston Public Schools
P.O. Box 3242
Houston, Texas 70007

Dear Dr. Vallejo:

In a recent conversation with C. J. Smith, Principal at Houston East High
School, I learned of your search for a Senior High Principal at South
Houston Metro High School. Please consider me a candidate for this position
and send me a formal application packet.

My varied administrative experiences are detailed on the enclosed résumé, but
I wish to point out that my experiences include working with a bilingual
student body and staff both in the United States and abroad. Currently, I
am the Secondary Principal of the American School of Quito, Ecuador, a
school of 2,750 students. The American School of Quito offers a standard
U.S. curriculum and is staffed by American teachers. The student body is
largely American (70%) with the remaining students representing Ecuador and
various other countries.

While I was on the administrative staff at Mesa, Arizona, I served as leader
of the South Central Association visitation team evaluating Johnson and
Roosevelt Junior High Schools in 1982. Because of this experience, I feel
knowledgeable about administrative procedures for the Houston Public Schools
and I feel that my background and experience with bilingual education would
permit me to make a strong contribution as an administrator of South Houston
Metro High School.

I will be returning to the Phoenix area in mid-June, and I could arrange to
interview in Houston at your convenience. If further information is needed,
please feel free to contact me. I look forward to your reply.

Sincerely yours,

Veronica R. George

Enc.

The reentry résumé prepared by Veronica George follows the same pattern as her overseas résumé (see page 45), but the résumé has been expanded to include a Professional Activities page. Key elements of the résumé (addresses, education and employment history, certifications, and references) are presented on the first page and, indeed, the first page could stand alone. In describing her current leadership responsibilities, Veronica has taken care to emphasize that the school has many similarities to a typical school in the States. Realizing that her past teaching and administrative positions are important to screening committees and hiring officials, brief annotations providing an overall picture of her varied experiences have been retained. Since many school districts request information about certificates held, Veronica has added this category to her résumé. Travel experiences have been updated, and, for the employer's convenience, the name of her university placement office has been added.

The Professional Activities page serves as a complement to the basic résumé. Veronica has designed this page to emphasize her capabilities and achievements as an educational leader. The four categories provide a clear and complete picture of her activities and involvements in education—in particular, her oral communication skills; her participation in community-related programs; her accomplishments in developing, promoting, and maintaining school curricular programs; her organizational and writing skills; and her interest in professional associations.

A significant feature of the combination of a basic résumé and a Professional Activities page is the greater flexibility it provides. The basic résumé can always be sent with a cover letter; the Professional Activities page can be included, modified, or rearranged to emphasize selected aspects of the applicant's background appropriate to the particular job description. The format, paper stock, and production method of the Professional Activities page should match the basic résumé, but the page need not be numbered.

Veronica George's letter of application is directed toward a specific position. The first paragraph informs the reader of her interest in the particular position, tells how she learned of the vacancy, and requests application materials.

The body of the letter effectively summarizes Veronica's experiences both in the United States and abroad, with an emphasis on the similarities of her previous positions to the position for which she is applying. Her letter clearly points out that she is bilingual and has experience with a bilingual student body and staff. In addition, Veronica is able to demonstrate some familiarity with two schools in the district.

The concluding paragraph indicates Veronica's plans to return to the Southwest and that she will be available for interviews at any time after returning to the United States.

INTERVIEWING FOR STATESIDE JOBS

Along with preparing the preliminary paper tools, some thought should be given to refreshing interview skills and preparing appropriate questions and responses. In all interview situations, educators should expect questions about previous experiences. Educators returning from a foreign assignment should also be fully prepared to discuss their motivations for going abroad, the nature of the overseas experience, and their motivations for returning to the United States. The typical stateside hiring official is aware of American-related overseas schools but may seldom have had the opportunity to interview applicants with recent foreign experience. The initial reaction is usually one of interest and curiosity, and the questions may tend to focus on the novelty of living abroad. Educators need to be aware of this likelihood and should be prepared to stress the educational relevance of the overseas experience, to bring up similarities of the curriculum and of the student body and staff, and to relate the foreign experience to previous stateside educational positions and responsibilities.

Educators should also be prepared for some naiveté and provincialism if the hiring official is not widely traveled. William Duermyer, a teacher formerly employed in the Middle East, notes that some stateside interviewers he encountered upon his return were under the impression that he had been working in one-room schools and that the curriculum was vastly different from that of most American schools. Preinterview planning and preparation will permit the applicant to guide the interview along positive and constructive lines so that relevant topics are adequately discussed and the interviewer understands both the nature and relevance of the overseas experience. For a discussion of stateside interviewing techniques and practices as well as other aspects of a stateside job search, educators may find it helpful to consult a previous publication by the authors, *From Contact to Contract: A Teacher's Employment Guide*.

READJUSTING TO THE UNITED STATES

Just as the arrival in a foreign country is a unique experience for each educator, so is the experience of reentering the United States. The degree to which individuals are affected by the return is obviously influenced by the difference in climate, life-style, and customs between the overseas location and the United States, but, to a greater or lesser extent, educators should expect to spend some time in readjusting to their own country.

Philip Houseal recorded in his journal his reactions shortly after having come home from Peru: "I'm depressed. I prepared myself for two months to come back home, and when I arrived I discovered there was nothing to be prepared for. Nothing seems as exciting as I thought it would."

Philip's reactions upon returning to the United States are not uncommon. Culture shock in a foreign country generally is anticipated to some degree, but the reentry culture shock may come as quite a surprise. Because the United States environment is a familiar one, reentry culture shock is usually of short duration, but its effects can be immediate and severe.

Adjusting to Materialism

Educators who have been away from the United States for two or more years may experience negative reactions to the obvious displays of American materialism. Kathryn Duermyer remembers: "Because we returned at Christmas time, I was particularly shocked by the wide variety of consumer products available. I spent hours in grocery stores in wide-eyed amazement at all the convenience foods available and at their relative cheapness compared to groceries in the Middle East." John Clayton, who had been working in Africa, experienced a similar reaction: "I recall feeling dizzy and puzzled when entering grocery stores." Such reactions to the overwhelming pervasiveness of American material wealth, however temporary they may be, are quite common among returning educators who had successfully adapted to a simpler way of life in a foreign country.

Adjusting to Family and Friends

Perhaps one of the most surprising and frustrating aspects of reentry is the discovery of an unexpected distance on the part of friends or family members. J. Chris Anderson's return from Zaire prompted these comments: "I had a great deal of difficulty conversing with my family and former friends, for it seemed that my experiences created a barrier between us. They asked me to describe my life there, but in doing so I began to realize that they lacked the experience to make my descriptions meaningful to them. We were living in separate worlds."

Educators at all levels advise returning teachers not to expect to be asked penetrating or in-depth questions about their experiences by acquaintances or even by close friends and family members. Professionals who have had extensive foreign experience understand that those who are not widely traveled may simply not have the background to share or inquire about the experience in a way that would be satisfying to the returning educator. Having spent several years teaching abroad, Karen Leonard offers this useful advice to returning educators: "Going abroad was a learning experience, but so is returning. Remember that the foreign experience was essentially yours, but others had growing experiences, too, and you will not necessarily understand them or be able to relate to the growing that friends and relatives have done in your absence. Not everyone is ecstatically interested in knowing about you. Be interested in what happened to them; you already know what happened to you."

Feeling Homesick

Many educators who have returned to the United States after a lengthy absence report that the combination of readjusting to the American life-style and the feeling of not being able to share experiences with family and friends produces a vague and undefined feeling of uneasiness. Often, it is only after some time has elapsed that these feelings are recognized as a "homesickness" for the host country. Routines of daily living that developed over time in the foreign environment—going to sidewalk cafes in the evening, shopping in bazaars and outdoor markets, and the leisurely pace of everyday activities—have suddenly been altered. Frequent opportunities to travel to fascinating locations, either alone or with fellow faculty members, may no longer present themselves. Travel opportunities within the States may seem to lack the novelty, glamour, and excitement of travel in foreign settings. Also, teachers in the United States are less likely than educators working together in a foreign country to join each other on travel jaunts. The camaraderie that existed among faculty members abroad is seldom found in the United States. Similarly, educators and their dependents may feel that the closeness of the relationship they shared during the international experience may have dissipated upon returning home because of the greater range of activities now available to each member of the family. The problems of readjustment may be compounded by the business aspects of resettlement and the pressures of a job search.

Unlike the educator who is newly arrived in a foreign setting, in which fellow staff members have undergone similar adjustments and can understand and empathize with the newcomer's problems, the returning educator is without a comparable support group and typically must work through the readjustment period alone. It may be helpful at this point for the returning educator to recall the period of adjustment to the foreign setting and the tactics employed in dealing with culture shock. Educators coming home should not be reluctant to try the coping strategies that worked for them while abroad.

After an extended absence, it is natural to experience feelings of alienation from one's own culture. A successful reentry requires an understanding that just as one had to forfeit or leave behind a part of oneself when moving to the foreign country, one must also let go of the past upon coming home. Some educators may attempt, with varying degrees of success, to retain or incorporate some of the changes in their personal life-style, but, as Karen Leonard points out: "You are, and will continue to be, an American. Refusing to recognize one's personal heritage and downgrading or disparaging things American while building up the foreign experience is romantic, unrealistic, and often detrimental."

LASTING EFFECTS

Whether one has been abroad for two years or ten, the effects of the international experience will endure for a lifetime. The intrinsic value of expanding one's horizons is not measured in terms of time or money but in internal growth and development. The satisfaction of knowing that personal and professional challenges have been met, that goals have been attained, and that lifelong friendships have been established will remain along with the innumerable memories of the overseas experience. John Stiles, a teacher in Brussels, eloquently expresses the thoughts and feelings of the majority of educators who have invested a portion of their lives in international education: "Living in a foreign culture has added a whole new perspective to my life. I have seen that there are many things people can learn from each other and incorporate into their own lives to make them fuller. Speaking another language has also greatly enriched my life. The experiences of my travels have broadened my mind, and my contacts with people from around the world have made me more sensitive to the global aspect of humanity. I am fortunate that I have known the experience of being a citizen of the world rather than of just one of its corners."

Appendix I

Useful Publications

INFORMATION SOURCES FOR OVERSEAS OPPORTUNITIES

Careers in International Affairs. School of Foreign Service, Georgetown University, Washington, D.C. 20057. 1982.

The Chronicle of Higher Education. The Chronicle of Higher Education, 1333 New Hampshire Avenue, N.W., Washington, D.C. 20036. Weekly. Subscriptions available from: The Chronicle of Higher Education, P.O. Box 1955, Marion, Ohio 43306.

Commonwealth Universities Yearbook. Association of Commonwealth Universities, John Foster House, 36 Gordon Square, London WC1H 0PF, England. Annual.

Congressional Directory. U.S. Government Printing Office, Washington, D.C. 20042. Annual.

Directory of the European Council of International Schools. European Council of International Schools, 19 Claremont Road, Surbiton, Surrey KT6 4QR, England. Annual.

Inter-Ed. Association for the Advancement of International Education, Room 200, Norman Hall, College of Education, University of Florida, Gainesville, Florida 32611. Monthly.

International Handbook of Education Systems. John Wiley & Sons, 605 Third Avenue, New York, New York 10158. 1983.

International Handbook of Universities. Macmillan Press, 4 Little Essex Street, London WC2R 3LF, England. Triennial.

ISS Directory of Overseas Schools. International Schools Services, P.O. Box 5910, Princeton, New Jersey 08540. Annual.

157

The London Times Education Supplement and *The London Times Higher Education Supplement*. Times Newspapers, Ltd., Priory House, St. John's Lane, London EC1M 4BX, England. Weekly.

The Overseas List. David M. Beckmann and Elizabeth Anne Donnelly. Augsburg Publishing House, 426 South Fifth Street, Minneapolis, Minnesota 55405. 1979.

Peterson's Annual Guide to Independent Secondary Schools. Peterson's Guides, P.O. Box 2123, Princeton, New Jersey 08540. Annual.

Schools Abroad of Interest to Americans. Porter Sargent Publications, 11 Beacon Street, Boston, Massachusetts 02108. Quadrennial.

World Guide to Universities. R. R. Bowker Co., 1180 Avenue of the Americas, New York, New York 10036. 1982.

World List of Universities. Macmillan Press, 4 Little Essex Street, London WC2R 3LF, England. Triennial.

The World of Learning. Europa Publications, 18 Bedford Square, London WC1B 3JN, England. Annual.

INFORMATION SOURCES FOR STATESIDE OPPORTUNITIES

Boarding Schools. Committee on Boarding Schools, 4 Liberty Square, Boston, Massachusetts 02109. 1981.

The Chronicle of Higher Education. The Chronicle of Higher Education, 1333 New Hampshire Avenue, N.W., Washington, D.C. 20036. Weekly. Subscriptions available from: The Chronicle of Higher Education, P.O. Box 1955, Marion, Ohio 43306.

Community, Junior, and Technical College Directory. American Association of Community and Junior Colleges, One Dupont Circle, Suite 410, Washington, D.C. 20036. Annual.

Comparative Guide to American Colleges. James Cass and Max Birnbaum. Harper & Row Publishers, 10 East 53rd Street, New York, New York 10022. Biennial.

Directory for Exceptional Children. Porter Sargent Publications, 11 Beacon Street, Boston, Massachusetts 02108. Biennial.

Directory of Public School Systems in the U.S. Association for School, College and University Staffing, Box 4411, Madison, Wisconsin 53711. Annual.

Education Week. Editorial Projects in Education, Suite 560, 1333 New Hampshire Avenue, N.W., Washington, D.C. 20036. Weekly.

The Executive Educator. The Executive Educator, 1055 Thomas Jefferson Street, N.W., Washington, D.C. 20007. Monthly.

From Contact to Contract: A Teacher's Employment Guide. Rebecca Anthony and Gerald Roe. The Carroll Press Publishers, P.O. Box 8113, Cranston, Rhode Island 02920. 1982.

Higher Education Directory. Higher Education Publications, 1302 18th Street, N.W., Suite 401, Washington, D.C. 20036. Annual.

Independent Schools. National Association of Independent Schools, 18 Tremont Street, Boston, Massachusetts 02108. Quarterly.

Peterson's Annual Guides to Graduate and Undergraduate Study. Peterson's Guides, P.O. Box 2123, Princeton, New Jersey 08540. Annual.

Peterson's Annual Guide to Independent Secondary Schools. Peterson's Guides, P.O. Box 2123, Princeton, New Jersey 08540. Annual.

Research Centers Directory. Gale Research Co., Book Tower, Detroit, Michigan 48226. Biennial.

Appendix II

A Selected List of Foreign Embassies, Information Services, and Diplomatic Missions in the United States

AFGHANISTAN
Embassy of Afghanistan
2341 Wyoming Avenue, N.W.
Washington, D.C. 20008

ALBANIA, People's Republic of
Permanent Mission of the
People's Republic of
Albania to the U.N.
250 East 87th Street
New York, New York 10028

ALGERIA
Embassy of Algeria
2118 Kalorama Road, N.W.
Washington, D.C. 20008

ANTIGUA-BARBUDA
Antigua-Barbuda Tourist Board
101 Park Avenue
New York, New York 10017

ARAB REPUBLIC OF EGYPT
Embassy of the Arab Republic
of Egypt
2310 Decatur Place, N.W.
Washington, D.C. 20008

ARGENTINE REPUBLIC
Embassy of the Argentine
Republic
1600 New Hampshire Avenue,
N.W.
Washington, D.C. 20009

ARUBA
Aruba Information Center
576 Fifth Avenue
New York, New York 10036

AUSTRALIA
Embassy of Australia
1601 Massachusetts Avenue, N.W.
Washington, D.C. 20036

Australian Consulate News and
Information Bureau
636 Fifth Avenue
New York, New York 10020

AUSTRIA
Embassy of Austria
2343 Massachusetts Avenue, N.W.
Washington, D.C. 20008

Austrian Institute
11 East 52nd Street
New York, New York 10022

BAHAMAS
Embassy of the Bahamas
600 New Hampshire Avenue,
N.W.
Washington, D.C. 20037

BAHRAIN
Permanent Mission of the State
of Bahrain to the U.N.
747 Third Avenue
New York, New York 10017

BANGLADESH
Embassy of Bangladesh
2123 California Street, N.W.
Washington, D.C. 20008

BARBADOS
Embassy of Barbados
2144 Wyoming Avenue, N.W.
Washington, D.C. 20008

Barbados Tourist and
Development Board
800 Second Avenue, 17th Floor
New York, New York 10017

BELGIUM
Embassy of Belgium
3330 Canfield Street, N.W.
Washington, D.C. 20008

Belgium Consulate-General
50 Rockefeller Plaza
New York, New York 10020

BELIZE (See United Kingdom)

BERMUDA (See United Kingdom)

BHUTAN
Permanent Mission of Bhutan
for the U.N.
866 Second Avenue
New York, New York 10017

BOLIVIA
Embassy of Bolivia
1145 19th Street, N.W., Suite 213
Washington, D.C. 20036

BOTSWANA, Republic of
Embassy of the Republic
of Botswana
4301 Connecticut Avenue, N.W.
Washington, D.C. 20008

BRAZIL
Brazilian Embassy
3006 Massachusetts Avenue, N.W.
Washington, D.C. 20008

BULGARIA, People's Republic of
Embassy of the People's Republic
of Bulgaria
2100 16th Street, N.W.
Washington, D.C. 20009

BURMA, Union of
Embassy of the Union of Burma
2300 S Street, N.W.
Washington, D.C. 20008

BURUNDI, Republic of
Embassy of the Republic
of Burundi
2717 Connecticut Avenue, N.W.
Washington, D.C. 20008

(CAMBODIA) Khmer Republic
Embassy of the Khmer Republic
4500 16th Street, N.W.
Washington, D.C. 20011

CAMEROONS, Federal Republic of
Embassy of the Federal Republic
of the Cameroons
2349 Massachusetts Avenue, N.W.
Washington, D.C. 20008

CANADA
Embassy of Canada
1746 Massachusetts Avenue, N.W.
Washington, D.C. 20036

Consulate General of Canada
Press and Information Service
251 Avenue of the Americas
New York, New York 10014

CENTRAL AFRICAN REPUBLIC
Embassy of the Central
African Republic
1618 22nd Street, N.W.
Washington, D.C. 20008

CHAD, Republic of
Embassy of the Republic of Chad
1132 New Hampshire Avenue, N.W.
Washington, D.C. 20037

CHILE
Embassy of Chile
1736 Massachusetts Avenue, N.W.
Washington, D.C. 20036

CHINA, People's Republic of
Liaison Office of the People's
Republic of China
2300 Connecticut Avenue, N.W.
Washington, D.C. 20008

COLOMBIA
Embassy of Colombia
2118 Leroy Place, N.W.
Washington, D.C. 20008

CONGO, Republic of
Permanent Mission of the Republic
of the Congo to the U.N.
801 Second Avenue
New York, New York 10017

COSTA RICA
Embassy of Costa Rica
2112 S Street, N.W.
Washington, D.C. 20008

CUBA
Permanent Mission of Cuba
to the U.N.
6 East 67th Street
New York, New York 10021

CYPRUS
Embassy of Cyprus
2211 R Street, N.W.
Washington, D.C. 20008

CZECHOSLOVAK Socialist Republic
Embassy of the Czechoslovak
Socialist Republic
3900 Linnean Avenue, N.W.
Washington, D.C. 20008

DAHOMEY, Republic of
Embassy of the Republic
of Dahomey
2737 Cathedral Avenue, N.W.
Washington, D.C. 20008

DENMARK
Embassy of Denmark
3200 Whitehaven Street, N.W.
Washington, D.C. 20008

Danish Information Office
280 Park Avenue
New York, New York 10017

DOMINICAN REPUBLIC
Embassy of the Dominican Republic
1715 22nd Street, N.W.
Washington, D.C. 20008

ECUADOR
Embassy of Ecuador
2535 15th Street, N.W.
Washington, D.C. 20009

EL SALVADOR
Embassy of El Salvador
2308 California Street, N.W.
Washington, D.C. 20008

EQUATORIAL GUINEA
Chargé d'Affaires, Equatorial Guinea
440 East 62nd Street, Apt. 6D
New York, New York 10022

ESTONIA
Legation of Estonia
Office of the Consulate General
9 Rockefeller Plaza
New York, New York 10020

ETHIOPIA
Embassy of Ethiopia
2134 Kalorama Road, N.W.
Washington, D.C. 20008

FIJI
Embassy of Fiji
1629 K Street, N.W., Suite 520
Washington, D.C. 20006

FINLAND
Embassy of Finland
1900 24th Street, N.W.
Washington, D.C. 20008

Finnish National Travel Office
505 Fifth Avenue
New York, New York 10017

FRANCE
Embassy of France
2535 Belmont Road, N.W.
Washington, D.C. 20008

French Cultural Services
972 Fifth Avenue
New York, New York 10021

GABON, Republic of
Embassy of the Republic of Gabon
2210 R Street, N.W.
Washington, D.C. 20008

GERMANY, Federal Republic of
Embassy of the Federal Republic
of Germany
4645 Reservoir Road, N.W.
Washington, D.C. 20007

German Information Center
410 Park Avenue
New York, New York 10022

GHANA
Embassy of Ghana
2460 16th Street, N.W.
Washington, D.C. 20009

GREECE
Embassy of Greece
2221 Massachusetts Avenue, N.W.
Washington, D.C. 20008

Greek Information Service
69 East 79th Street
New York, New York 10021

GREENLAND (see Denmark)

GUATEMALA
Embassy of Guatemala
2220 R Street, N.W.
Washington, D.C. 20008

GUINEA
Embassy of Guinea
2112 Leroy Place, N.W.
Washington, D.C. 20008

GUYANA
Embassy of Guyana
2490 Tracy Place, N.W.
Washington, D.C. 20008

HAITI
Embassy of Haiti
4400 17th Street, N.W.
Washington, D.C. 20011

HONDURAS
Embassy of Honduras
4715 16th Street, N.W.
Washington, D.C. 20011

HONG KONG
Hong Kong Tourist Association
548 Fifth Avenue
New York, New York 10036

HUNGARIAN PEOPLE'S REPUBLIC
Embassy of the Hungarian People's
Republic
2437 15th Street, N.W.
Washington, D.C. 20009

ICELAND
Embassy of Iceland
2022 Connecticut Avenue, N.W.
Washington, D.C. 20008

INDIA
Embassy of India
2107 Massachusetts Avenue, N.W.
Washington, D.C. 20008

Indian Consul General
3 East 64th Street
New York, New York 10021

INDONESIA, Republic of
Embassy of the Republic
of Indonesia
2020 Massachusetts Avenue, N.W.
Washington, D.C. 20036

IRAN
Embassy of Iran
3005 Massachusetts Avenue, N.W.
Washington, D.C. 20008

IRAQ
Embassy of Iraq
1801 P Street, N.W.
Washington, D.C. 20036

IRELAND, Republic of
Embassy of the Republic of Ireland
2234 Massachusetts Avenue, N.W.
Washington, D.C. 20008

ISRAEL
Embassy of Israel
1621 22nd Street, N.W.
Washington, D.C. 20008

ITALY
Embassy of Italy
1601 Fuller Street, N.W.
Washington, D.C. 20009

Italian Cultural Institute
686 Park Avenue
New York, New York 10021

IVORY COAST, Republic of
Embassy of the Republic of
Ivory Coast
2424 Massachusetts Avenue, N.W.
Washington, D.C. 20008

JAMAICA
Embassy of Jamaica
1666 Connecticut Avenue, N.W.
Washington, D.C. 20009

Consulate General of Jamaica
Information Service
200 Park Avenue
New York, New York 10017

JAPAN
Embassy of Japan
2520 Massachusetts Avenue, N.W.
Washington, D.C. 20008

Japan Information Service
235 East 42nd Street
New York, New York 10017

Japan Foundation
600 New Hampshire Avenue, N.W.
Suite 430
Washington, D.C. 20037

JORDAN, Hashemite Kingdom of
Embassy of the Hashemite
Kingdom of Jordan
2319 Wyoming Avenue, N.W.
Washington, D.C. 20008

KENYA
Embassy of Kenya
2249 R Street, N.W.
Washington, D.C. 20008

KOREA, Republic of
Embassy of the Republic of Korea
2320 Massachusetts Avenue, N.W.
Washington, D.C. 20008

Korea Travel Service
Barr Building, Suite 527
910 17th Street, N.W.
Washington, D.C. 20006

KUWAIT
Embassy of the State of Kuwait
2940 Tilden Street, N.W.
Washington, D.C. 20008

LAOS
Embassy of Laos
2222 S Street, N.W.
Washington, D.C. 20009

LATVIA
Legation of Latvia
4325 17th Street, N.W.
Washington, D.C. 20011

LEBANON
Embassy of Lebanon
2560 28th Street, N.W.
Washington, D.C. 20008

LESOTHO, Kingdom of
Embassy of the Kingdom of Lesotho
1601 Connecticut Avenue, N.W.
Washington, D.C. 20009

LIBERIA
Embassy of Liberia
5201 16th Street, N.W.
Washington, D.C. 20011

LIBYAN ARAB REPUBLIC
Embassy of the Libyan Arab
Republic
2344 Massachusetts Avenue, N.W.
Washington, D.C. 20008

LITHUANIA
Legation of Lithuania
2622 16th Street, N.W.
Washington, D.C. 20009

LUXEMBOURG
Embassy of Luxembourg
2210 Massachusetts Avenue, N.W.
Washington, D.C. 20008

MACAO (see Portugal)

MALAGASY REPUBLIC
Embassy of the Malagasy Republic
2374 Massachusetts Avenue, N.W.
Washington, D.C. 20008

MALAWI
Embassy of Malawi
2362 Massachusetts Avenue, N.W.
Washington, D.C. 20008

MALAYSIA
Embassy of Malaysia
2401 Massachusetts Avenue, N.W.
Washington, D.C. 20008

MALDIVES, Republic of (see
Sri Lanka)

MALI, Republic of
Embassy of the Republic of Mali
2130 R Street, N.W.
Washington, D.C. 20008

MALTA
Embassy of Malta
2017 Connecticut Avenue, N.W.
Washington, D.C. 20008

MARTINIQUE (see France)

MAURITANIA, Islamic Republic of
Embassy of the Islamic Republic
of Mauritania
2129 Leroy Place, N.W.
Washington, D.C. 20008

MAURITIUS
Embassy of Mauritius
4301 Connecticut Avenue, N.W.
Washington, D.C. 20008

MEXICO
Embassy of Mexico
2829 16th Street, N.W.
Washington, D.C. 20009

MONACO
Monaco Government Tourist Office
610 Fifth Avenue
New York, New York 10020

MONGOLIAN PEOPLE'S REPUBLIC
Permanent Mission of the Mongolian
People's Republic to the U.N.
6 East 77th Street
New York, New York 10021

MOROCCO
Embassy of Morocco
1601 21st Street, N.W.
Washington, D.C. 20009

MUSCAT and OMAN, Sultanate of
Embassy of the Sultanate of Muscat
and Oman
2342 Massachusetts Avenue, N.W.
Washington, D.C. 20008

NAURU
Consul of Nauru
110 Sutter Street
San Francisco, California 94104

NEPAL
Embassy of Nepal
2131 Leroy Place, N.W.
Washington, D.C. 20008

NETHERLANDS
Embassy of the Netherlands
4200 Linnean Avenue, N.W.
Washington, D.C. 20008

NETHERLANDS ANTILLES
Netherlands Antilles Windward
Islands
Tourist Information Office
4 West 58th Street
New York, New York 10019

NEW ZEALAND
Embassy of New Zealand
19 Observatory Circle
Washington, D.C. 20008

NICARAGUA
Embassy of Nicaragua
1627 New Hampshire Avenue, N.W.
Washington, D.C. 20009

NIGER, Republic of
Embassy of the Republic of Niger
2204 R Street, N.W.
Washington, D.C. 20036

NIGERIA
Embassy of Nigeria
1333 16th Street, N.W.
Washington, D.C. 20036

NORWAY
Embassy of Norway
3401 Massachusetts Avenue, N.W.
Washington, D.C. 20007

Norwegian Information Service
290 Madison Avenue
New York, New York 10017

PAKISTAN
Embassy of Pakistan
2315 Massachusetts Avenue, N.W.
Washington, D.C. 20008

PANAMA
Embassy of Panama
2862 McGill Terrace
Washington, D.C. 20008

PARAGUAY
Embassy of Paraguay
2400 Massachusetts Avenue, N.W.
Washington, D.C. 20008

PERU
Embassy of Peru
1700 Massachusetts Avenue, N.W.
Washington, D.C. 20036

PHILIPPINES
Embassy of the Philippines
1617 Massachusetts Avenue, N.W.
Washington, D.C. 20036

POLISH PEOPLE'S REPUBLIC
Embassy of the Polish People's
    Republic
2640 16th Street, N.W.
Washington, D.C. 20009

PORTUGAL
Embassy of Portugal
2125 Kalorama Road, N.W.
Washington, D.C. 20008

Portuguese National Tourist
    and Information Office
570 Fifth Avenue
New York, New York 10036

QATAR
Embassy of Qatar
2721 Connecticut Avenue, N.W.
Washington, D.C. 20008

RÉUNION (see France)

RHODESIA
Rhodesia Information Office
2852 McGill Terrace
Washington, D.C. 20008

ROMANIA, Socialist Republic of
Embassy of the Socialist Republic
    of Romania
1607 23rd Street, N.W.
Washington, D.C. 20006

RWANDA, Republic of
Embassy of the Republic of Rwanda
1714 New Hampshire Avenue, N.W.
Washington, D.C. 20009

SAN MARINO
Consul of San Marino
400 Madison Avenue
New York, New York 10017

SÃO TOME (see Portugal)

SAUDI ARABIA
Embassy of Saudi Arabia
1520 18th Street, N.W.
Washington, D.C. 20036

Saudi Arabia Information Bureau
866 United Nations Plaza,
    Room 527
New York, New York 10017

SENEGAL, Republic of
Embassy of the Republic of Senegal
2112 Wyoming Avenue, N.W.
Washington, D.C. 20008

SEYCHELLES (see United Kingdom)

SIERRA LEONE
Embassy of Sierra Leone
1701 19th Street, N.W.
Washington, D.C. 20009

SINGAPORE, Republic of
Embassy of the Republic
    of Singapore
1824 R Street, N.W.
Washington, D.C. 20009

SOMALI DEMOCRATIC REPUBLIC
Embassy of the Somali Democratic
    Republic
1875 Connecticut Avenue, N.W.,
    Suite 1109
Washington, D.C. 20009

SOUTH AFRICA, Republic of
Embassy of the Republic
    of South Africa
3051 Massachusetts Avenue, N.W.
Washington, D.C. 20008

South African Information Service
635 Madison Avenue, 14th Floor
New York, New York 10021

SPAIN
Embassy of Spain
Office of the Cultural Counselor
2700 15th Street, N.W.
Washington, D.C. 20009

SRI LANKA
Embassy of Sri Lanka (Ceylon)
2148 Wyoming Avenue, N.W.
Washington, D.C. 20008

SUDAN, Republic of
Embassy of the Republic of Sudan
3421 Massachusetts Avenue, N.W.
Washington, D.C. 20007

Consulate General of the Republic
of Sudan
757 Third Avenue
New York, New York 10017

SWAZILAND
Embassy of Swaziland
4301 Connecticut Avenue, N.W.
Washington, D.C. 20008

SWEDEN
Embassy of Sweden
600 New Hampshire Avenue, N.W.
Washington, D.C. 20008

Swedish Information Service
825 Third Avenue
New York, New York 10022

SWITZERLAND
Embassy of Switzerland
2900 Cathedral Avenue, N.W.
Washington, D.C. 20008

SYRIAN ARAB REPUBLIC
Permanent Mission of the Syrian
Arab Republic to the U.N.
964 Third Avenue
New York, New York 10022

TAIWAN
Taiwan Coordination Council
for North American Affairs
Information and Communications
Division
4301 Connecticut Avenue, N.W.
Washington, D.C. 20008

Chinese Information Service
159 Lexington Avenue
New York, New York 10016

TANZANIA, United Republic of
Embassy of the United Republic
of Tanzania
2010 Massachusetts Avenue, N.W.
Washington, D.C. 20036

THAILAND
Embassy of Thailand
2300 Kalorama Road, N.W.
Washington, D.C. 20008

TOGO, Republic of
Embassy of the Republic of Togo
2008 Massachusetts Avenue, N.W.
Washington, D.C. 20008

TRINIDAD and TOBAGO
Embassy of Trinidad and Tobago
2209 Massachusetts Avenue, N.W.
Washington, D.C. 20008

TUNISIA
Embassy of Tunisia
2408 Massachusetts Avenue, N.W.
Washington, D.C. 20008

TURKEY, Republic of
Embassy of the Republic of Turkey
1606 23rd Street, N.W.
Washington, D.C. 20008

UGANDA, Republic of
Embassy of the Republic of Uganda
5909 16th Street, N.W.
Washington, D.C. 20011

UNION OF SOVIET SOCIALIST
REPUBLICS
Embassy of the Union of Soviet
Socialist Republics
1125 16th Street, N.W.
Washington, D.C. 20036

UNITED ARAB EMIRATES
Embassy of the United Arab
Emirates
600 New Hampshire Avenue, N.W.,
Suite 740
Washington, D.C. 20037

UNITED KINGDOM (of Great Britain
and Northern Ireland)
Embassy of Great Britain
3100 Massachusetts Avenue, N.W.
Washington, D.C. 20008

British Information Services
845 Third Avenue
New York, New York 10022

UPPER VOLTA, Republic of
Embassy of the Republic
of Upper Volta
5500 16th Street, N.W.
Washington, D.C. 20011

URUGUAY
Embassy of Uruguay
1918 F Street, N.W.
Washington, D.C. 20006

VENEZUELA
Embassy of Venezuela
2445 Massachusetts Avenue, N.W.
Washington, D.C. 20008

VIET NAM, Republic of
Embassy of the Republic
of Viet Nam
2251 R Street, N.W.
Washington, D.C. 20008

WESTERN SAMOA
Honorary Consul, Western Samoa
P.O. Box 39818
Los Angeles, California 90039

YEMEN ARAB REPUBLIC
Embassy of the Yemen Arab
Republic
600 New Hampshire Avenue, N.W.
Washington, D.C. 20037

YUGOSLAVIA
Embassy of Yugoslavia
2410 California Street, N.W.
Washington, D.C. 20008

Yugoslav Information Center
488 Madison Avenue
New York, New York 10022

ZAIRE REPUBLIC
Embassy of Zaire Republic
1800 New Hampshire Avenue, N.W.
Washington, D.C. 20009

ZAMBIA, Republic of
Embassy of the Republic of Zambia
2419 Massachusetts Avenue, N.W.
Washington, D.C. 20008

Appendix III

Teacher Certification Offices in the United States

ALABAMA
Certification Section
State Department of Education
Room 349, State Office Building
501 Dexter Avenue
Montgomery, Alabama 36130
(205) 832-3133

ALASKA
Teacher Certification Office
State Department of Education
Pouch F, Alaska Office Building
Juneau, Alaska 99811
(907) 465-2831

ARIZONA
Certification Division
Arizona Department of Education
1535 West Jefferson
Phoenix, Arizona 85007
(602) 255-4367

ARKANSAS
Teacher Education and Certification
State Department of Education
Little Rock, Arkansas 72201
(501) 371-1474

CALIFORNIA
Commission for Teacher
  Preparation and Licensing
1020 O Street
Sacramento, California 95812
(916) 445-7254

COLORADO
Division of Teacher Education
  and Certification
Colorado Department of Education
Room 310, State Office Building
201 East Colfax Avenue
Denver, Colorado 80203
(303) 839-3075

CONNECTICUT
Teacher Certification Unit
Connecticut Department
  of Education
P.O. Box 2219
Hartford, Connecticut 06115
(203) 566-2670

DELAWARE
Certification and Personnel
  Division
State Department of Public
  Instruction
Townsend Building
Dover, Delaware 19901
(302) 678-4686

DISTRICT OF COLUMBIA
District of Columbia
  Public Schools
415 12th Street, N.W.
Washington, D.C. 20004
(202) 724-4279

FLORIDA
Teacher Education, Certification,
and Staff Development
Department of Education
Tallahassee, Florida 32301
(904) 488-1234

GEORGIA
Teacher Certification
Georgia Department of Education
209 State Office Building
Atlanta, Georgia 30334
(404) 656-2604

HAWAII
Office of Personnel Services
State Department of Education
P.O. Box 2360
Honolulu, Hawaii 96804
(808) 548-6384

IDAHO
Teacher Education and Certification
State Department of Education
Len Jordan Office Building
Boise, Idaho 83720
(208) 334-3475

ILLINOIS
Teacher Certification
Illinois Office of Education
100 North First Street
Springfield, Illinois 62706
(217) 525-3774

INDIANA
Teacher Education and Certification
Department of Public Instruction
Room 229, State House
Indianapolis, Indiana 46204
(317) 633-4759

IOWA
Teacher Education and Certification
Division
Department of Public Instruction
Grimes State Office Building
Des Moines, Iowa 50319
(515) 281-3245

KANSAS
Accreditation and Certification
State Department of Education
Kansas State Education Building
120 East 10th Street
Topeka, Kansas 66612
(913) 296-2288

KENTUCKY
Council on Teacher Education
and Certification
Kentucky Department of Education
1823 Capital Plaza Tower
Frankfort, Kentucky 40601
(502) 564-4606

LOUISIANA
Higher Education and Teacher
Certification
State Department of Education
P.O. Box 44064
Baton Rouge, Louisiana 70804
(504) 342-3490

MAINE
Department of Educational and
Cultural Services
Division of Certification and
Placement
Augusta, Maine 04333
(207) 289-2441

MARYLAND
Division of Certification and
Accreditation
Maryland Department of Education
P.O. Box 8717
Baltimore-Washington International
Airport
Baltimore, Maryland 21240
(301) 796-8300

MASSACHUSETTS
Teacher Preparation, Certification,
and Placement Bureau
Massachusetts Department
of Education, Room 630
31 St. James Avenue
Boston, Massachusetts 02116
(617) 727-5726

MICHIGAN
Teacher Preparation and Certification
Services
Michigan Department of Education
106 West Allegan
Lansing, Michigan 48909
(517) 373-3310

MINNESOTA
Personnel Licensing and Placement
Minnesota Department of Education
Capitol Square Building
550 Cedar Street
St. Paul, Minnesota 55101
(612) 296-2046

MISSISSIPPI
Teacher Certification
State Department of Education
Sillers State Office Building,
Suite 802
P.O. Box 771

Jackson, Mississippi 39205
(601) 354-6869

MISSOURI
Teacher Education and Certification
State Department of Education
Jefferson City, Missouri 65101
(314) 751-3486

MONTANA
Certification and Teacher Education
Office of Public Instruction
1300 Eleventh Avenue
Helena, Montana 59601
(406) 449-3150

NEBRASKA
Certification and Teacher Education
Nebraska State Department
of Education
301 Centennial Mall South
Lincoln, Nebraska 68509
(402) 471-2496

NEVADA
Teacher Education and Certification
Nevada Department of Education
400 West King Street
Carson City, Nevada 89701
(702) 885-5700

NEW HAMPSHIRE
Teacher Education and Professional
Standards
Department of Education
State House Annex
Concord, New Hampshire 03301
(603) 271-2407

NEW JERSEY
Teacher Education and Academic
Credentials
New Jersey Department of Education
225 West State Street
Trenton, New Jersey 08625
(609) 292-4477

NEW MEXICO
Teacher Education and Certification
State Department of Education
Education Building
Santa Fe, New Mexico 87503
(505) 827-2789

NEW YORK
Division of Teacher Education
and Certification
State Education Department
State Education Building
31 Washington Avenue
Albany, New York 12234
(518) 474-3901

NORTH CAROLINA
Division of Teacher Education
Standards and Certification
State Department of Public
Instruction
Education Building
Raleigh, North Carolina 27611
(919) 733-4125

NORTH DAKOTA
Certification
State Department of Public
Instruction
State Capitol
Bismarck, North Dakota 58505
(701) 224-2264

OHIO
Division of Teacher Education
and Certification
State Department of Education
Ohio Departments Building,
Room 1012
Columbus, Ohio 43215
(614) 466-3593

OKLAHOMA
Teacher Certification Section
State Department of Education
Oliver Hodge Memorial Education
Building
Oklahoma City, Oklahoma 73105
(405) 521-3337

OREGON
Teacher Education and Certification
Oregon Department of Education
700 Pringle Parkway, S.E.
Salem, Oregon 97301
(503) 378-3569

PENNSYLVANIA
Bureau of Certification
Department of Education
333 Market Street
P.O. Box 911
Harrisburg, Pennsylvania 17108
(717) 787-2967

RHODE ISLAND
Teacher Education/Certification
Department of Education
199 Promenade Street
Providence, Rhode Island 02908
(401) 277-6835

SOUTH CAROLINA
Teacher Education and Certification

Department of Education
1015 Rutledge Building
1429 Senate Street
Columbia, South Carolina 29201
(803) 758-5081

SOUTH DAKOTA
Teacher Certification
State Department of Public
Instruction
Kneip Office Building
Pierre, South Dakota 57501
(605) 773-3553

TENNESSEE
Teacher Education and Certification
State Department of Education
123 Cordell Hull Building
Nashville, Tennessee 37219
(615) 471-1644

TEXAS
Teacher Certification
Texas Education Agency
201 East Eleventh Street
Austin, Texas 78701
(512) 475-2721

UTAH
Certification
Utah State Board of Education
250 East Fifth South
Salt Lake City, Utah 84111
(801) 533-5965

VERMONT
Teacher Certification Section
State Department of Education
Montpelier, Vermont 05602
(802) 828-3135

VIRGINIA
Teacher Certification
Department of Education
Richmond, Virginia 23216
(703) 786-5300

WASHINGTON
Certification/Licensing
Office of the Superintendent
of Public Instruction
Old Capitol Building
7510 Armstrong Street, S.W., FG 11
Tumwater, Washington 98504
(206) 753-6773

WEST VIRGINIA
Educational Personnel Certification
State Department of Education
Building 6, Capitol Complex
Charleston, West Virginia 25305
(304) 348-7017

WISCONSIN
Teacher Certification
Bureau of Teacher Education
and Certification
State Department of Public
Instruction
125 South Webster Street
Madison, Wisconsin 53702
(608) 266-1027

WYOMING
Division of Certification, Placement,
and Teacher Education
State Department of Education
Cheyenne, Wyoming 82002
(307) 777-7673

Index